HOME

A PHILOSOPHY OF
PERSONAL SPACE

MEL THOMPSON

Brimstone Press

ACKNOWLEDGEMENTS

I would like to thank:

Nicolas Wyatt, whose work on the sacred geography of the ancient Near East set me thinking.

Nigel Rodgers, whose wise editorial advice helped me to re-shape an earlier draft of this book.

Philip Painter, who kindly went through the manuscript with his professional, proofreading eye.

Keith Walton, founder of the self-publishing co-operative, Brimstone Press, for enabling the book to find its home.

Members of Hertfordshire Writers, a local group of the Society of Authors, for their on-going encouragement.

Finally, none of this would have been possible without the indulgence and support of my wife, Marianne, who, as always, is also my first reader.

First published by Brimstone Press
www.brimstone-press.com

© Mel Thompson, 2021
ISBN 978 1 906 38563 7

The concept of 'home' reflects one of the deepest and most universal of human experiences. It manifests in everything from religion to nationalism, and from the desire to personalise where we live, to nostalgia for the place of our birth, or commitment to particular people, places and ideas.

This book invites you to take a journey, reflecting on self and home, identity and belonging.

Contents

...

Introduction

... all really inhabited space bears the essence of the notion of home.

Gaston Bachelard [1]

Home. The idea is so universal and intuitively obvious that we seldom feel the need to reflect on what it means. But its absence or presence, and its power to distort or seduce, shapes our lives.

This book will argue that a sense of 'home' lies at the centre of the idea of 'personal space', of the way in which we understand our world in personal terms.

Although it's difficult to define, we all know what it means to feel 'at home'. To be back after a trip and see the old familiar place as if for the first time, or to discover in some far-flung location a place to which we feel instinctively drawn, a place that is homely for us, where we suddenly think 'yes, I could happily live here'. Or, at the extreme, to imagine with the poet Rupert Brooke the distant resting place of a fallen soldier: 'That there's some corner of a foreign field/That is forever England'.[2] That grave, even in the desolate killing fields of 1914, takes on a new character, infused with a significance that speaks of home.

Home is fundamental to human flourishing and a key concept for understanding the significance of personal space – the sense of belonging, on personal, social and political levels. It is the basis of personal identity; it gives motivation; it provides a sense of security in an ever-changing world.

But what home means for each of us is not always obvious. It is not just a particular place, let alone the place where we were born, but includes people, values, ideas and commitments. Home is where we belong, wherever that may be. Above all, home is the axis around which our personal world moves, the central point on the map that shows us both where we are and who we are.

Consider two contrasting situations: to feel 'at home', surrounded by the familiar, accepted, belonging, centred, loved; to feel lost, confused, without direction or meaning, surrounded by the unfamiliar or alien, rootless, without support, isolated and shunned. These evoke deep emotional responses, but they are not just about emotions; they are about how we understand our world. They do not so much describe a place as the relationship I have with it. Nor are they static. My old sense of home may be shattered by the tragedy of loss, or betrayal, or the natural urge to grow up and move on. Equally, I may gradually come to appreciate the place in which I now feel lost; I may yet make friends, settle down, establish a new home.

Our world is too often impersonal, competitive and isolating. Whether it's during a war, a natural disaster, an economic crisis or the disruption caused by a pandemic, we sense the powerlessness of being subject to forces that are utterly beyond our control. Within the routine of life, we become consumers, customers or citizens, subject to the competitive chances and threats of a capitalist world, or the repressive restrictions of an authoritarian one. In response, people tend to divide their life between the personal – family, friends, places that are thought of as 'home' – and the more impersonal world of work, politics and social change, but then struggle to achieve a work/life balance.

Is your first image of home a romantic one? The welcome at a cottage door? The smell of baking bread? The garden in which to potter? The seat in which to sit to contemplate life? It may indeed be all of these, but home is more than a place, real or imagined; it is the essence of your personal space, gathering in a single concept the people, places, hopes, fears, ideas and values that have shaped your life.

Nagging in the background of life there may be a yearning for things to be settled, or different, or right. Although it may present itself as ambition, or fetish or passion or success, most people are just looking for a sense of home; they want to 'arrive'. Failing that, they tend to settle for money. But money can only buy stuff; it can't buy home. Status, professionalism, creativity – or perhaps belonging to a close-knit circle of people, each reinforcing the other's quest – are not just substitutes for home, they create a form of home, a circle, a belonging, a sense of purpose, of meaning. Society shapes up a home in the form of interlocking relationships, as a bird weaves twigs into its nest.

Taking to politics or religion is another form that the quest for home can take. Bringing together beliefs, experiences and shared loyalties, religious or political groups may entice us with a sense of belonging. But we may find ourselves asking: 'do I belong here because I accept all these beliefs and values, or do I accept them because I want to belong here?'

Does religion make sense of the idea of home? Or does home make sense of the idea of religion? The religious question, in a secular culture, is not 'what do you believe?' but 'where do you belong?'

If lost in a website I try to return to the 'home' page to get my bearings; if the computer malfunctions, I turn it off and on again to reset it and start over. Life has no reset button; but, if it did, its reset would be to 'home'.

Be clear about one thing, to avoid disappointment. If you have never felt self-doubt, or wondered how it is that your life has shaped up the way it has, or longed to feel a fundamental certainty that could give it meaning, then this book is probably not for you. Nor will it offer you easy answers. The shaping of personal space is a process that is unique to each one of us, requiring honesty and some hard thinking.

PERSONAL SPACE

Science is based on observation and reason; it attempts to understand and describe space and time in a detached, objective way. It has yielded such useful results that we may assume it to be the only way of understanding our world.

However, people need more than an impersonal description. They need to encounter the world in ways that give life meaning, to find places where they naturally belong, and people with whom they are happy to identify.

We all need space to be ourselves, but we need it to be the kind of space that we can personalise – space that says something about who we are. In this book, I shall be exploring the idea that, as we go through life, we create a personal map of value and meaning, superimposed over our experience of the world. Some places are important to us – they speak of home or evoke special memories – others are impersonal and cold. The same applies to times; our birthday is not like any other day, even if, for everyone else, it is *exactly* that.

But this is not what is usually meant by 'personal space'. In *The Hidden Dimen*sion, 1969, the cultural anthropologist Edward T. Hall, used the term proxemics for 'the interrelated observations and theories of man's use of space as a specialized elaboration of culture' Mainly concerned with communication, he spoke of the intimate and personal distances, up to about four feet (1.2 metres), within which we are happy to allow close friends and those with whom we are intimate. Outside that zone, we have social space and public space. Since then, most discussion of 'personal space' has been concerned with how we guard ourselves in crowded situations, requiring a certain distance between ourselves and strangers, and feeling threatened if crushed up against other people.

Psychology and anthropology have thus explored the way in which we create and guard our personal space, with implications for urban density and design. They have noted cultural difference in the sort of personal space that people need, with some people (e.g. the Japanese) being far happier in close proximity than others (e.g. British or Americans).

The implication of such anthropological studies is that, if you understand personal space, you will be better able to communicate with others in a way that they do not see as threatening or aggressive. By contrast, this book – in taking a broader definition of personal space – suggest that, if you reflect on the importance for you of where you belong, you will be able to build a sense of inner security, and will therefore be less likely to try to use other people to give you a sense of identity, less needy in relationships and more willing to share. Those who are emotionally homeless are always on the lookout for something to satisfy their inner lack.

THE NEED FOR HOME

A sense of home is something to be cultivated, reflected on and cherished. We are constantly changing, but change is best effected from a position of awareness – so knowing our 'home' is not to be limited to it, but perhaps also to understand why we may want to move on.

Nature is a web of things and events, ever-changing, ambiguous, unpredictable. Habitually, we see things in terms of discreet events or entities; we identify and place them within a frame of reference. That process is evidence-based, analytic and rational, but it does not do justice to our actual experience of life, which is more value-laden, personal, intuitive and immediate.

A home is not the same thing as a shelter. It goes without saying that people need a place where they can shelter, giving them security and privacy. We tend to refer to those who live on the streets as 'homeless' and so they are. But their fundamental need is for shelter. Whether that shelter subsequently becomes a 'home', or whether they choose to make a temporary home out on the street, is another matter. We are right to be concerned about those who are physically homeless. Most are thrust into that sad position through circumstances over which they have only limited control. It goes without saying that they need to be housed. My argument here, however, is that their plight is but the tip of an iceberg, the bulk of which is an insidious depersonalisation of our life and the relationship we have with our environment. Our task is to explore that elusive something that turns a shelter into a home.

Beware those who claim to be cosmopolitan but are effectively homeless and rootless, especially if they are wealthy and superficially successful. The rootless are not to be trusted, for they are vulnerable to the inordinate appeal of abstract concepts such as wealth, power or revenge.

Homo sapiens displays a remarkable degree of restlessness. Unlike ruminating animals, apparently content with their immediately presented meal and the prospect of quietly chewing the cud, we generally only chew the cud in order to devise a plan that will change our world, to propel ourselves from the here and now into a planned-for future. If our life is a narrative, then our quest is to shape our story towards an ending that might make sense of all that we have been and done.

TWO RESPONSES

Throughout this book we shall be exploring ways in which people deal with the idea of home and the threat of emotional homelessness. This is not just an intellectual question, but a personal and practical one. In general, it seems that there are two very different approaches, but whether one is inherently better than the other is for you to decide.

One response is to work at creating a home. This may involve personalising the space around us, so that it expresses our values and commitments and becomes uniquely our own. It may also involve accepting ideas, ideologies or values that help us to gel with like-minded people. If we want to belong, we join a group, make relationships and get involved.

The other tendency, which we can see in some who offer meditation as a route to success, or promote the international, cosmopolitan lifestyle of the self-made, is to attempt to get beyond the need for any sense of home. On a recent camping

15

trip in the USA, I spotted an RV with a sticker on the back saying 'Home is where we've parked it!' Like the original cosmopolitan, the Cynic Diogenes, I might choose to declare that I belong to no particular *polis*, or city, but that the universe itself is my *polis* – that I am utterly *cosmopolitan*. Those following that tendency are happy to move to wherever they find the best living conditions or lowest taxes, comfortable with the idea that they can shift around the world on a whim, owing no permanent or exclusive allegiance to any nation, creed or culture.

So we either go on a quest to construct a home, or we try to live without one, and between those two fundamental positions there are any number of possibilities. There may be times when we need to branch out, to move away from a previous home, to try something new – even to the extent of trying to set up several different homes at once, at work, perhaps, or socially, or even in terms of a new interest or hobby. At other times, feeling somewhat lost, adrift or living without a clear goal, we may need to get to grips with who we are and where we belong. A new home, a new family, a new job: there are many ways in which people try to settle into a new sense of themselves.

Beyond a certain age, it is also possible for us to look back on our life, incredulous that we were indeed the same person who lived back then, with such a different set of ideas, hopes and dreams, not to mention that younger body. Did I really do that? What must I have been thinking of? Why did I choose that career? Or that partner? Or that cause? Life changes; we change. Nothing remains the same from birth to death, other than the name we are given, and even that can be changed legally. There is continuity, of course, without which our social life would be utterly chaotic and our identity problematic. But change is unavoidable, and the developing and re-drawing of a map of values, along with a re-shaping of the sense of home that lurks within us, suggests where we belong at our present stage in life.

EMOTIONS AND UNDERSTANDING

Personal space deserves a philosophy, because it needs to be related to the way we think, not just to how we feel. To be 'lost' or 'at home' are contrasting emotional states, but they are also contrasting cognitive states. At the moment of feeling lost, our usual sense of orientation – of knowing where we are because we recognise things that are familiar – breaks down. We are threatened, because we cannot get an intellectual handle on the territory in which we find ourselves. We do not *understand* where we are. By contrast, to *know* that we are 'at home' suggests that we can relax; our surroundings are familiar; we are comforted by the signals that our senses provide for us.

Sand dunes stretch to the horizon. How we feel as we survey them depends on whether we are lost, with diminishing supplies of water and tortured by the sun, or enjoying the sight as part of a vacation. Untamed nature remains a threat, but one that is modified by our social networks.

In any 'user group', like-minded people get together, share their enthusiasm, use a common language, and often disparage any who appear to come in from the outside without understanding the language or assumptions of the *cognoscenti*. To belong is also to know, to understand, to grasp the concepts that enable us to navigate our world, however large or small that world may be. If you don't believe me, just

17

join a couple of Facebook-groups. There is an unspoken wealth of knowledge and exclusivity hidden within each contribution. The newcomer stands out, as lacking the cognitive assumptions of the rest. To get to belong, you also need to understand how to find your way around.

So being 'at home' or having a personal space is not simply a matter of emotional attachment, but of having cognitive underpinnings. Hence, this is a 'philosophy' of personal space, not simply an emotional description of its benefits.

THE STRUCTURE OF OUR ARGUMENT

This book falls into three parts:

1. In the first three chapters we shall look at the existential impact of the vast, impersonal universe revealed by modern cosmology, the way in which we cope with this by constructing and mapping out personal worlds of meaning and value, and then at how the resulting idea of personal space changes the way we understand ourselves, both in terms of neuroscience and experience.

2. The next two chapters survey the cognitive, cultural and religious maps that shaped people's views of the world before the challenge presented by modern science and cosmology, and the way in which an exclusively rational and scientific view may distort our world.

3. Finally, we have four chapters that examine the ways in which people create a sense of home and personalise the space around them, the philosophy of personal engagement, the implications all this has for society and politics, and finally the way in which the quest for home can be presented in terms of a personal and spiritual journey.

We shall be looking at the experience of personal space, from the design of ancient temples, through the impact of Greek thought, medieval religion and the rise of science, to some twentieth century thinkers who sought to understand experience in a way that went beyond the conventional gulf between subjective experience and objective fact. And, since the experience of home reflects the way we relate reason and analysis to the more intuitive elements of value and meaning, we shall need to look at some recent findings of neuroscience and particularly the relationship between the right and left hemispheres of the brain.

Home is not a place, but a relationship. It describes how we think and feel about places, people, groups and ideas. It locates them in the centre of our web of values; it affirms them as giving our life meaning.

I shall argue that our understanding of home, and our experience of personal space, can only be appreciated and enhanced if we allow our reason and our intuition to inform one another. We shall be exploring the relationship between feeling at home and thinking about who we are and where we really belong.

A CONFESSION AND AN INVITATION

Nietzsche claimed every book to be a secret autobiography. We reveal ourselves, not just by what we write, but especially why we write it. Inevitably, therefore, this book will have its autobiographical elements. For me, the sense of where I belong has always been problematic, reflecting conflicting loyalties and loves. The argument presented here is therefore also part confession, part invitation to join me on a personal journey.

I remember sitting on a riverbank in the Essex village of my birth, one bright August morning, vaguely aware of the chirping of moorhens dabbling among the reeds and the drone of a harvester in the nearly field. I was eighteen and, perhaps for the first time, had been struggling to know what I should do with my life. But, as I sat there, I began to sense that I could happily surrender myself to the bank, sink down into its soil and be absorbed into a comfortable nothingness. With all my life before me, I felt that I could happily die there and then. I had set out to ask myself where I wanted to go in life, but found the answer in the strange but comfortable feeling that, somehow, I had already arrived. Moments passed, perhaps half an hour, and yet time meant nothing. I was held in the centre of things: the quiet place amid the world's cacophony; a still point, around which the world spun. I felt reluctant to return to the ordinary messiness of life. I wanted to hold on to that moment of clarity, sensing something of profound importance, but for which I found no words.

Over the intervening years, I have often longed to regain that sense of 'home' but have seldom found it. I've gone back many times to that same stretch of bank, and sat, and waited, but nothing has happened. Every experience has its time, and its unique impact on our lives. It sets up a longing that can probably never be satisfied. It tells us who we are; it speaks of 'home'.

This is the spot where, for the first time, I consciously experienced the sense of being 'at home'. Where's yours?

20

This book is therefore an invitation to explore; to reflect on self and home, identity and belonging. It suggests that a sense of home may be used as an interpretive key to unlock some of the problems of self, brain and identity and also give a new perspective on the old problem of how the self is related to the world, science to religion and our perceptions to the reality we assume we perceive.

Although a work of philosophy, it is inevitably personal, for without a personal and unique perspective – yours and mine – our perceptions easily become fossilised and trapped in logical questions that permit no satisfactory answers.

When thought becomes blocked, only the Zen-like clapping of a hand will do. When the world appears imprisoned by determinism or the self by neural necessity, only a sense of personal space can free us.

This is not a book for those who think they have arrived, but for those who know that they are still travelling, reflecting on where they truly belong, and striving to make the world a 'home'. It swings between exploring the more general sense of personal space and the specific idea of 'home'; neither makes sense without the other.   However, it is the intuition of 'home' that introduces us to the more general issue of how we encounter and interpret the spaces within which we find ourselves.

Finding our way home is a unique and personal journey. But come with me now, and let us reflect together on what it has meant to be 'at home', from the ancient Near East, through the guidelines offered by religion, philosophy and culture, to the present-day conflicts and confusions in a world where we need to identify, but are offered too many choices, and where localism and nationalism vie with cosmopolitan, multi-ethnic, multi-racial blending, and where people are defined as much by their aspirations as by their origins.

Human flourishing demands that we know where we belong. It is a question from which we cannot escape, but which requires of us both sensitivity and smart thinking.

Our argument starts, back in the nineteenth century, with a voice warning of a world that it had lost its way ...

Chapter 1

The Breath of Empty Space

Has it not become colder? Is not night continually closing in on us?
Do we not feel the breath of empty space?

Friedrich Nietzsche, *The Joyful Wisdom*

The universe revealed by modern cosmology is vast, impersonal and threatening. Within it, our habitable space is insignificant and temporary, no more than a thin film of blue and green over the surface of the planet. But worse, even within this rare film of life and as a member of its dominant species, it is all too common to find our sense of personal significance and value threatened, when we are treated as no more than a vote, a number, a consumer or a statistic. We need to feel 'at home', but today's world – both cosmic and social – doesn't make that easy.

This chapter opens with a quote from Nietzsche. Ideas that have been brewing intellectually for decades may find dramatic expression in a single paragraph. So it was that, in the nineteenth century, as science was continuing to shatter former certainties, Nietzsche famously presented the image of a madman crying out 'God is dead'. That might have been remarkable enough, but what the madman said next was darker, more chilling, and provides the starting point for our discussion:

Who gave us the sponge to wipe away the whole horizon? What did we do when we unchained this earth from its sun? Where is it moving now? Where are we moving? Away from all suns? Is there still an 'above' and 'below'? Are we not wandering as through an endless nothingness? Has it not become colder? Is not night continually closing in on us? Do we not feel the breath of empty space?[3]

Gone, for Nietzsche, were the boundaries that allowed the world to give moral and metaphysical certainty. In their place he proclaimed the rise of the Übermensch, or superman, the next step in our evolutionary progress. For him, self-affirmation was to provide direction and meaning in a universe that offered neither. He demands that we take responsibility for our own destiny, meaning and value; he argues that we, humanity, are to become the meaning of the Earth.

In another context that might have seemed liberating. After all, Nietzsche is challenging us to make more of ourselves, to move towards the Übermensch, but that progress cannot be easy or its results assured, for we are invited to chart our own future in a world that is radically directionless.

Why is that so chilling? Because it threatens one of the deepest and most essential features of human happiness: the sense of 'home' – of belonging, of having a place in the overall scheme of things. Our fundamental need is for a place of shelter; our deepest fear, to be lost or cast out as a homeless wanderer. Even if we pretend self-sufficiency, we may secretly know it to be a sham and long to be provided with the emotional comforts of home.

Hence, the complaint of Nietzsche's madman that the horizon has been wiped away. Today, secular cosmology does not offer us the benefit of being set in the fixed centre of things, surrounded by providential spheres. There is no up or down in our world, unless we choose to declare it to be so. But if value and direction are determined by our own choices, rather than provided by the structure or God-given design of the universe, we become vulnerable to the values imposed upon us by others.

When something goes wrong, we usually try to find someone to blame. But what if everything that happens is pre-determined and completely out of our hands? What if we are all lost through no fault of our own? In the absence of God, with whom might we lodge our complaint? Is there an alternative to existential despair, given that nothing lasts? How can we create for ourselves a 'home' in the midst of empty space? Is the sense of 'home' an essential feature of human consciousness, without which we are diminished, or a futile, illusory craving?

COSMIC ANGST

Like it or not, the world remains stubbornly impersonal. Whether it is the long-term fate of a galaxy or the arrival of a new virus, our understanding of ourselves needs to take into account that which stands over against us in all its threatening power

I am not interested in just taking another look at the dimensions of the universe – that is both unnecessary for our argument and beyond my competence – but rather, I want to explore how cosmology makes us *feel* and how it relates to our sense of home. How, given what we know of the size and impersonal nature of the universe, can we feel 'at home' in it without intellectual compromise?

An imaginative contemplation of the universe stuns the mind. We live on a planet whose sun is out on a limb. Thirty two thousand light years from the centre of our spiral galaxy, itself one of hundreds of billions, speeding away from us at unimaginable speeds across a void. To make things worse, our knowledge of the size of the universe continues to change at an astounding rate. It was only in 1923 that Edward Hubble first observed a galaxy; today we estimate that there are 200 billion of them, each with an average of 200 billion stars. Even the millions of light years that separate us from our nearest neighbouring galaxy[4] reinforce the sense that, from the perspective of modern cosmology, we are confined to a tiny speck of blue hopelessly lost in the blackness of space. Cosmology is not for agoraphobics!

The destructive and creative forces within the universe are equally impressive. One of the most remarkable photographs of a cosmic event shows the explosion of the star Eta Carinae, more than 8,000 light years away. Massive clouds of dust and gas, measuring about half a light-year across, streak outwards at 1.5 million miles per hour. The event is primarily of interest to us because we, and everything we know around us, are built of material forged in such cosmic explosions.

Our planet is therefore fragile and temporary, made possible by the warmth and gravitational pull created by the sun, itself a modest star that presents the most astoundingly hostile of environments, burning 600 million tons of hydrogen each and every second.

In a universe such as this, we delude ourselves if we claim to be masters of our own destiny. Any attempt at an objective view of our place in the universe sends the mind reeling, a void opens, and we face the stark truth of nothingness. Can such a universe ever feel like a home?

BROOKLYN AND THE UNIVERSE

There is a wonderful moment in Woody Allen's film *Annie Hall* when the young Allen character is taken by his mother to see the doctor because he is depressed. Asked why he feels that way, he mumbles 'The universe is expanding'. Clearly, for him that single fact drains everything of meaning and value, since everything is coming apart. His mother complains that he won't even do his homework. 'What's the point?' he shrugs. 'What's the universe got to do with it?' she replies. 'You're here in Brooklyn. Brooklyn is not expanding.' The doctor takes another approach. 'It's been expanding for billions of years ... We can just enjoy ourselves while we can.'

Those two answers to the boy's unconscious response to Nietzsche's challenge could not be more different. The first denies that what we know about the universe applies locally: God is not dead; there has been no sponge; the horizon is still where it always was; there's a church on the corner of the street, so all's well. The second shifts to the existential: the universe is impersonal, expanding and meaningless, but – hey – let's just make the most of what we have here and now.

Feeling the breath of empty space, we may indeed ask 'What's the point?' So I want to explore the responses given to the question posed by Woody Allen's character.

First of all, we need to face up to the facts, however uncomfortable they may make us feel. Modern cosmology is largely the quest for a mathematical model by which we can interpret the various features of the observed universe. Behind this approach is the assumption that human rationality, expressed in the application of mathematical logic to the data of experience, is capable of understanding and predicting the world in which we live.

But constructing mathematical models – however brilliant – does not answer questions about human value and purpose, and we should not expect it to. All we need to do at this stage is guard against cognitive dissonance. In other words, the basis on which we make our decisions, whether individual or global, should not go against the body of established facts that are the background to modern life.

So how do we relate the universe to Brooklyn? We somehow need to scale down a universal fact – in this case expansion – to take into account its local impact. In this sense, both the boy and his mother are correct. The fact of universal expansion, applied literally to the human scale, suggests that 'What's the point?' is a realistic response. But if something is happening over billions of years, need it concern us? Perhaps his mother is right in claiming that 'Brooklyn in not expanding', since its expansion is below any detectable threshold and the boy's existential crisis – even if imaginatively justified by contemplating the universe – is not going to solve the issues of his homework or living his life in Brooklyn.

The boy's response is not unique. The Catholic scientist and theologian, Pierre Teilhard de Chardin, argued that, without some definite end point to evolution, humankind would simply give up in disgust, sapped of all energy and enthusiasm for the future.[5] He needed direction; he needed structure. He was, of course, brought up as a good Catholic, schooled in the theology of Thomas Aquinas and committed to making his home within the Jesuit order. Exiled to China, when his thoughts were judged heretical, he was painfully excluded from his natural homes, in France and with the Jesuits. Although he compensated by establishing for himself a new home within the scientific community, the pain of his original loss never left him. As it happened, he died, still in exile, not far from Brooklyn.

In practice, most people simply bypass uncomfortable cosmic facts and get on with applying energy and enthusiasm to what is more local and immediate – the doctor's response, which we shall explore a little later.

Or perhaps the universe would feel more homely if we simply gave up trying to understand it. But that would require us to put a barrier between how we choose to see our proximate world and what we know of the universe as a whole, and we hit the problem of cognitive dissonance – trying to hold together incompatible facts. That approach cannot be satisfactory, because ultimately it is the universe at large that will decide our fate, and there remains one fact that we cannot (literally) avoid, which threatens to link the universe to Brooklyn ...

AN ENCOUNTER WITH EROS

To assume that modern cosmology deals with matters so abstract and vast that they can have no impact on life on earth require us to turn a blind eye to an inescapable fact about the objects that make up the universe: from time to time, they collide.

Planets are regularly bombarded with material from space. We hardly notice, as small meteors enter Earth's atmosphere each day, depositing tonnes of extra-terrestrial debris on the surface. Mostly they burn up as they enter the atmosphere; larger ones are seen from earth as 'shooting stars' and meteor showers occur annually when we pass through trails of debris.

Sometimes a larger object comes close to Earth. In 1937, an asteroid called Hermes, one mile in diameter, crossed our orbit just six hours before we reached that spot. The Hale–Bopp comet was seen passing us in February and March 1997, at a distance of a mere 123 million miles, and Toutaris – an asteroid almost three miles across at its widest – passed less than four lunar distances from the earth in 2004.

There are an estimated 100,000 near-earth asteroids of sufficient size to do serious damage. When it comes to the threat of incoming bodies, size is everything. Meteorites are small chunks of stone or iron, and they arrival frequently. Objects that are less than about 50 yards in diameter, generally break up and burn in the upper atmosphere, but occasionally an object is large enough to survive the plunge. On 30th June 1908 a chunk of debris about 50 yards in diameter exploded over Siberia, devastating 400 square miles of forest.

Let's get this into perspective. An incoming object of 100 yards diameter, is likely to arrive once every 10,000 years, destroying a considerable area or causing a tsunami, depending on its point of impact. If it were to be a mile in diameter, the whole climate would be affected, and the area of destruction would be several hundred miles in diameter, but that would likely happen only once in every 250,000 years. Go upscale to 10 miles in diameter and the chance of a collision is reduced to once every 100 million years, but it would cause a mass extinction of life on Earth. A large asteroid or comet is thought to have put an end to the dinosaurs some 65 million years ago, leaving a crater one hundred miles in diameter in the Yucatan peninsular in Mexico.

But then there is Eros ...

Eros is the name given to a chunk of rock; an asteroid, elongated in shape and up to 14 miles in diameter, famous not just for its size, but for being the first asteroid to be landed on by a robotic space probe.[6] Like a misshapen club, it turns and turns as it hurtles through space, its surface cratered by impacts with other debris. At the moment it circles the sun quite harmlessly between the orbits of Earth and Mars, but with each orbit it shifts very slightly under the gravitational influence of the planets. In 1996 a team from the University of Pisa calculated that, within a million years, there is a 50% chance that it will be nudged into Earth's orbit.

By the standards of most things that come our way, Eros is huge,[7] and its heaviness gives it added kinetic energy and destructive power. If the evidence of past encounters is anything to go by, the arrival of Eros, thundering in at many tens of thousands of miles per hour, would signal the end of humankind and probably most other species. It would be most unlikely that any living thing could survive either the trauma of the impact itself, or starvation as a result of the clouds of dust circling in the atmosphere for years, blotting out the sun and impeding the growth of plants. The threat of a 'nuclear winter', mooted in discussing the hazards of nuclear war, was negligible in comparison.

Coping with destruction by Eros is unlikely to be high on our agenda, for the collision, although imminent in astronomical time, is distant from a human perspective. But it draws

30

attention to two features of life: that the universe is more beautiful, vast and yet more violent than we can comprehend, and that, for most of the time, people are more concerned with Eros' namesake, the god of love, as they plan the structure of their lives. Human life is shaped by more immediate factors; by joys and fears, loves and hates. We approach an encounter with Eros blissfully unaware, engrossed in our own schemes for the future.

Some more distant events have a greater degree of certainty. So, for example, we know that our own Milky Way and the Andromeda galaxy are approaching each other at about 300,000 miles an hour. It is probable that they will eventually collide and merge. Yet it is unlikely to happen for another 5 billion years, and by that time, our sun will have gone through the phase of becoming a 'red giant', vaporising all life on Earth in the process. One way or another, our luck will eventually run out and life on Earth will cease.

So, to be realistic, our home needs to resemble a tent rather than a cave. It is always going to be out there, moveable, vulnerable to change. We cannot retreat into it as though we thereby arrive at a point at which all the hazards of life are finally avoided. In constructing our home, whether in a personal and family sense or globally, we need to recognise its temporary nature if we are not to be disappointed. As the Buddha declared: nothing lasts forever, and our futile hope that it will, is the root cause of suffering.

What's our time frame here? Should we be concerned for this generation only? For our children, or grandchildren? Where do we draw the line beyond which it make no difference to us what happens? This has immediate implications for our concerns about, for example, global warming. In order to act with integrity, we need to accept that our environment is worth cherishing and protecting, even though it is subject to radical change.

This suggests a moral imperative to help, protect and cherish even that which is, in a longer perspective, doomed. The fact that everyone will die one day does not render medical attention pointless. Nor, therefore, should we reject something as a 'home' simply because it cannot be unchanging or of eternal significance.

Therefore, to retain our integrity, our quest for 'home' is going to be rather more existential than scientific.

THE HORROR OF INDIFFERENCE!

The French existentialist philosopher Maurice Merleau-Ponty, coined the phrase 'the horror of indifference' to sum up what we face when we consider the dimensions of the universe. But he was far from being the first to describe this. In his *Pensées*, the seventeenth century mathematician and theologian Blaise Pascal said that the 'eternal silences of infinite space' terrified him. We need to look squarely at this horror of indifference if we are to understand its polar opposite, the feeling of being 'at home'.

The problem is that, with the arrival of Newtonian physics, space and time were seen as little more than a structure or a receptacle. Walter Benjamin, a German philosopher and cultural critic, spoke of the problem of dealing with 'homogenous, empty time' and the Canadian philosopher Charles Taylor[8] commented that:

> … time, like space, has become a container, indifferent to what fills it.

As we shall see later, this was utterly different from the earlier sense of an ordered and organised cosmos, as seen by thinkers from the ancient Greeks to Aquinas. Today, we do not sense that we live in an ordered *cosmos*, but only a *universe*. That may be fine in terms of scientific calculations, but it is not an environment within which we can happily feel at home.

Charles Taylor speaks of 'a nostalgia for transcendence'. That may not be the way everyone would express it, but there is a longing for a world that makes sense, within which we have a part to play, a world that is mapped out before us, with things to love and things to hope for, a world in which some sort of morality makes sense because the world is shot through with values to which we can subscribe.

Is this a naïve fantasy? An unconscious need? A nostalgic vision of a world long gone? Is it religious, or can it be enjoyed in entirely secular terms?

Finding an answer to these questions will make all the difference to how we understand our world. What we are searching for here is a way of seeing the world that relates both to our emotions and our intellect, for there is no turning back to a world prior to the rise of modern science.

Charles Taylor looked for a transformation beyond simple human flourishing, exploring belief in a transcendent reality. However, our aim here will be for something less, but more immediate. Human flourishing is no bad thing in itself! If it provides sensitivity and contentment, it may also start to tackle the greatest problem confronting humanity, namely our treatment of the environment. For intentions to be transmitted into action, we need to be both convinced about the need for a healthy and harmonious relationship with the environment, but also feel it as a *desired goal, not a compromise*, justified for itself, rather than forced on us by utilitarian considerations.

We face the horror of indifference, whether in the movement of galaxies, the multiplying of malignant cells within our own bodies, or the random selection of victims by an inanimate virus. The world is mostly unfair and impersonal. We would love it not to be so; to find it caring and benevolent; to be able, as might a young child, to ask the world to kiss it better when disease or warfare strike down those we love. But it is not so, and as adults we have to face the fact of human folly and fragility. But how, then, do we avoid cynicism? How can we make of this world a 'home' in which we can thrive and to which we can be committed?

THE COMFORT OF SCIENCE?

Not everyone would find his or her personal world threatened by the detached objectivity of science. For one thing, its very objectivity might detach us from our petty worries. That was certainly the view of the nuclear physicist Erwin Schrodinger, famous for his cat-in-a-box dilemma. He argued, in *What is Life?* (1944), that we need to stand back from our engagement with life in order to get an objective view. For us, as individuals, the most threatening thing is that one day we will die. But from an objective perspective our death is absolutely insignificant. That may be true, but it is not the way we would look at it most of the time.

For some, however, an understanding of the physical principles that govern the world can be profoundly comforting. At the end of his review of Tim Radford's *The Consolations of Physics* in 2018, Graham Farmelo comments:

> For me, the main joy of physics is that it puts human beings so firmly in their place. Even if every living thing died tomorrow, every quantum in the universe would carry on doing its eternal dance to fundamental laws that we shall probably never discover. If you're not a scientist, that thought might not be very consoling. But I'm just happy to keep on doing some physics.[9]

But the question remains … Can we feel 'at home' in a universe that is so vast and impersonal? To find comfort in the eternal operation of quarks, even when all human and other forms of life have vanished from the universe, is to have our taste buds enhanced by the driest of sherry!

THE EXISTENTIAL OPTION

Clearly, it's time to tell ourselves a more comforting story, or at least devise one for the children, in case they start to have nightmares. But we cannot give up on the quest to establish a 'home'. It is the deepest of human needs and a necessary component of our happiness, especially in a world where so many aspects of life can seem threateningly impersonal.

So what do we do if a virus strikes, the economy crashes, the political situation becomes chaotic and the future looks bleak? The answer appears to be that we focus on smaller worlds that offer comfort: gardening and homemaking; a shared style in dress or music; racial or national identity; the supposed certainties of fundamentalist religion or the commitment to a political ideology. Garden centres and DIY stores flourish, makeovers increase and property prices rise. We seek whatever appears to offer us the world on a manageable scale.

The quest for home may take on a nostalgic tinge. Would it be easier to feel 'at home' in a small town in the West of England? Perhaps, but what one person experiences as cosy, another may find claustrophobic. Community is not created instantly, but built up gradually, over the years.

We should not dismiss the satisfaction that comes from these, nor the most trivial of gestures – personalising our car by warping letters and numbers to spell out our name on the

35

registration plate – they may appear simplistic answers to a profound question, but they are at least a gesture in the right direction. After all, if people strive to be creative in the arts, or give themselves to a worthy cause, a profession, or a career, it may seem more elevated in terms of vocation, but they are also ways of being 'at home' within a community that gives us a sense of belonging. So we should not be snobbish about the means used to create a sense of home. Perhaps we should accept Jeremy Bentham's principle that, in assessing utilitarian benefits, 'the quantity of pleasure being equal, push-pin is as good as poetry'.

To construct a home in this way is not a matter of swapping an indifferent external, objective world for a personal and subjective one. Nor is a sense of home an anomaly in an otherwise rational or empirically defined world. Personal space is the *starting point* of our experience, not an optional extra. If what is fundamental and necessary appears questionable or even impossible, something must be wrong with the way we are thinking. Time, therefore, to consider a remarkable writer and existentialist outsider ...

CAMUS AND THE ABSURD

The French writer and existentialist philosopher Albert Camus[10] argued that life is 'absurd', not because it lacks personal meaning, or that it is material and random, but because there is a fundamental gulf between the impersonal world and our craving for meaning, purpose and explanation. We must have something we cannot have – we are designed to flourish only when provided with that which will be forever beyond our grasp.

Camus' sense of the absurd parallels Nietzsche's 'death of God'. For both of them, we are thrown into a world that does not fit our requirements and have to face the consequences. We seem to need a God, or at least for the world to make sense, but neither appears possible – that is the absurdity of our situation.

In *The Myth of Sisyphus* Camus describes the absurd as arising from the contrast between a meaningless world and our need for 'clarity and cohesion'.[11] Although Sisyphus continues to engage in the pointless task of continually pushing a boulder up a hill, only to have it roll down again, Camus comes to the view that perhaps Sisyphus is actually happy, even in an impersonal world without direction or purpose.

There is a parallel here with our consideration of 'home'. Consciously or unconsciously, we want, need and search for it, but – from the standpoint of science and cosmology – it appears forever beyond our grasp. In personalising space, creating and imposing upon our world a map of meaning and value, we seek to overcome this absurdity by creating a world that reflects our needs.

What we are exploring here on a personal level is familiar territory for social anthropologists such as Fiona Bowie who argued, in *The Anthropology of Religion* (Blackwell, 2000), that cosmology is fundamental to human societies. It orientates a community within its world, defines its identity, its place and its sense of belonging. Without a cosmology, individuals are adrift and society becomes dislocated.

But it's not just cosmology; it's statistics, big data, economics – all the impersonal factors that frustrate our lives. They distort the way we see things. Within an overall capitalist worldview, the environment is a resource, something there to provide what we need, waiting to be exploited. We do not identify with it, but over against it. Seen like that, the natural world is not a home, but a potential for energy or food. This is in contrast with Native American and other societies, where the natural environment is sacred and gives identity to the tribe. Those who are removed from it become lost, their lives drained of meaning.

But that's not just about economic systems or the anthropology of minority groups, it's hard wired into all of us. We need a sense of home in order to flourish. The universe as we know it today has set a new agenda, rendering obsolete most of our earlier ideas about the world and humankind's place within it. Sometimes a single moment or image can encapsulate both the longing for home and the beautiful vulnerability of life on earth. Captured on film as the spacecraft rounded the moon, the image, known as 'Earthrise', shows the beauty and colour of our planet, hanging in the distance, a jewel set against the blackness of space.

In cosmic terms, that is our world, our challenge and our home.

THE CHALLENGE

In the twenty first century, we cannot avoid the fact that, as a society, we long ago took the sponge and wiped away the horizon, refusing to conform to a traditional framework of meaning, but now find that we have also wiped away something essential to our own happiness. Beneath the much-misunderstood idea of 'God', whom Nietzsche's madman declared dead, there lay a more fundamental one: 'home'.

We need solid ground beneath our feet, even if we know that everything is shifting and changing. Nothing is permanent – a truth emphasised by the Buddha two and a half thousand years ago – and we grasp at permanence to our own peril. But impermanence is not the same thing as having no sense of personal space. It is perfectly possible to have a positive sense of who we are and where we belong, even as we know that both we, and everything we relate to, are in a constant process of change and will eventually cease to exist.

After all, we do not reject people just because they are growing and changing. Indeed, part of the delight in having children is watching them change and develop. If we tried to arrest that development, fixing them as a baby or infant when they are already past that stage, is to do them great harm. Love and let grow; love and embrace change; love through the tears brought on by the changes that we dreaded. Personal space will always be elusive; touched, sensed and gone.

Even in the most familiar of homes there are changes – a new child in the family, the changed décor, the move to a new house, a death – but they are generally balanced by the continuity of other elements. Breakdowns happen when too much is changed all at once. If you are made redundant, divorce and move home all at the same time, your health may suffer – unless, that is, you have some over-arching sense of self and direction that can accommodate all these things and still point the way forward.

On the most personal of levels, that is also a key feature of good relationships. Partners need to be sufficiently supportive to allow change while maintaining support – a centre that needs to hold, even when all else seems to be falling apart.

And yes, the reference here is to W. B. Yeats' 'The Second Coming', written in the aftermath of the First World War. Like Nietzsche's prophetic madman, Yeats depicts a world in which the assumptions and social structures of earlier generations no longer apply. The world is like the falcon, turning and turning as it rises beyond the point at which it can hear the voice of the falconer. As a result, 'mere anarchy is loosed upon the world' and then his famous observation 'things fall apart; the centre cannot hold.'

FACT OR FANTASY?

Is our sense of 'home' a valid way of interpreting our place in the universe, or is it an illusion, albeit a potentially therapeutic one? Are we in fact lost and directionless, but fooling ourselves with our sense of home?

Whether fantasy or reality, one thing is clear. In a crisis, when challenged to achieve a single, clearly defined goal, people find within themselves surprising resources of energy. So it is understandable that those who hope to persuade us that they have a recipe for a more fulfilled life tend to do just that – to get us to sort our priorities, to get a grip on what we really want, to have the courage to go by those values and goals and to make them come true for us. In other words, they suggest that the enfeebled 'lost' will find strength when they establish a 'home'.

But that promise of empowerment will only appear credible if it fits in with other beliefs that we hold. To retain integrity and avoid cognitive dissonance, each new belief needs to mesh naturally into our existing view of the world. If a belief is utterly at odds with our habitual understanding, we have three options: either we reject it, or we set aside all the previously assumed beliefs in order to accept it, or we try to hold both the background beliefs and the new one in a kind of creative (or destructive) tension.

The breath of empty space has posed a question about our personal space and sense of home. Are we repeating the mistake of which Marx accused religion – namely that we are making 'home' the heart of a heartless world, the opium of the people?

Are we regressing into childhood with our quest for home? Should we simply grow up and accept the world as it is, with all its vast, impersonal power? Perhaps. But people find it natural to rebel against an impersonal world, determined to find their own sense of direction and meaning. How they do so is the subject of our next chapter.

Chapter 2

Of the Making of Maps

No sooner had the warm liquid mixed with the crumbs touched
my palate than a shudder ran through me and I stopped,
intent upon the extraordinary thing that was happening to me.
An exquisite pleasure had invaded my senses ...

Marcel Proust

At the opening of *In Search of Lost Time*, Marcel Proust
describes lying awake in bed as a child, aware of the position
of his bed and of furniture in the room around him. He hears
the whistles of railway engines in the night, giving him a sense
of the dimension of the countryside beyond his room. He
comments:

> When a man is asleep, he has in a circle around him the
> chain of the hours, the sequence of the years, the order of
> the heavenly host. Instinctively, when he awakes, he looks
> to these, and in an instant reads off his own position on
> the earth's surface and the amount of time that has
> elapsed during his slumbers ...

And he describes the precise sequence of thoughts on waking
at midnight:

... when I awoke at midnight, not knowing where I was, I could not be sure at first who I was; I had only the most rudimentary sense of existence, such as may lurk and flicker in the depths of an animal's consciousness; I was more destitute of human qualities than the cave dweller; but then the memory, not yet of the place in which I was, but of various other places where I had lived, and might now very possibly be, would come like a rope let down from heaven to draw my soul out of the abyss of non-being, from which I could never have escaped by myself ...

And in this way he describes putting together the component parts of his ego. He knows *who* he is, because he becomes aware of *where* he is. The familiar walls take shape around him and he settles back in bed.

And this experience of disorientation happens also for those plagued with guilt, regret or recent bereavement – for a moment they may be distracted, perhaps by something on television, or a conversation, or a piece of music, and they feel content, but then, like a stab in the pit of the stomach, the reality returns, the familiar burden of life reinstates itself, and the distraction is recognised for what it is. Later, for the bereaved, the first experience of happiness may be laced with guilt. How could I have forgotten him?

In this way, things, situations or places, take on special meaning, reminding us of who we are, locating us within our world. That is precisely the phenomenon I want to explore: the relationship between the sense of self and the sense of place.

FROM INFANCY

The first experiences of a baby are vague, undifferentiated: breast, milk, satisfaction, or at least the cessation of the as yet unspecified pangs of hunger. Only gradually does she start to explore her world, of touch, warmth, belonging, food and then, bit-by-bit, of shapes that become familiar, of other people, of surroundings.

The granularity of that experiences increases, until the small child can look about, recognise, cry, seek what she wants, feel comfortable to be laid down, or wish to be picked up. At the same time, the world of the baby becomes differentiated into areas of value. This is welcome, that is not; this feels good, that is painful; this person is familiar and a source of comfort, that person is strange – smells wrong, looks wrong, makes the wrong sounds – and is to be avoided.

Over the next couple of years, the child crawls, then walks, knows her family, hates to be left alone, or can happily settle with toys in a corner. She hears a sound and looks in that direction, she looks to where the familiar person has gone, and toddles after them. She starts to speak, to communicate, to become aware of using a shared space.

And in doing so, she is establishing a sense of personal space, divided into the warm, friendly and familiar on the one hand, and the cold, strange and threatening on the other. She is starting to ask for things; she knows her needs and where to look to have them met. In other words, she starts to engage, in an increasingly sophisticated way, with the world.

The baby shuffles along, discovering that she does not need to wait for something to arrive, but can go and seek it out. She discovers that she can move around a room, eventually through a doorway and into a whole new space.

With the first steps the process accelerates and freedom beckons. The child laughs to find that she can run, can explore, can choose what is to hand. Life is no more a matter of waiting and crying and hoping that food will be provided; now there is action to be taken, shouting or crying to express need.

Few words suffice at this stage. A toddler in a buggy finishes one biscuit, and a hand reaches up and out to the side, anticipating that the adult doing the pushing will provide the same again. Just one word is needed and used for the first time – 'More!' The startled, bemused adult recognises that the child has learned something new, and hands over another biscuit. Thus we bring a sense of order and control to replace the helpless mystery of our early experiences.

The growing child is challenged to expand her personal space: into the play area with friends; into a nursery; into school; into activities with others; into knowing a special corner where toys and things are kept.

She learns to share, first screaming if a toy is taken away, then learning to resist that reaction. She becomes an individual to the extent that she learns how to behave with others.

But, of course, not all children have these things provided. Many are deprived of them through war, poverty or neglect, and we are rightly concerned that such deprivation will hinder their progress to maturity, simply because the way in which personal space is cultivated and enlarged is a necessary part of the process of growing up.

But it is not only children who may be deprived and at a disadvantage. An adult who has forgotten what it is like to enlarge, develop and share personal space, may develop a sense that the world is there only as something to be grabbed and used, a desperate source of comfort, or a constant threat.

Maturity is all about coming to terms with the variety of spaces within which we operate, and to handle them appropriately. Those who shout and grasp may be described as infantile, because they have not developed the skill of using and responding to what comes within their personal space.

THE EXPERIENCED VIEWPOINT
In this chapter we are concerned primarily with the actual experience we have of our personal space. How this relates to issues of brain, senses and identity will be covered later.

For now, however, we simply need to recognise that, behind my eyes, there is nothing but solid matter. But that's not how I experience myself as I look out into my world. I know that my experience can be described in terms of chemical and electrical activity in my brain, but that's not the same as seeing a world, or moving within it, aware of its threats or opportunities. I know that damage to my senses or brain will change my perception of the world. As someone who is developing cataracts in both eyes and is also profoundly deaf, I am all too aware that a sensory failure has an immediate and inescapable impact of how things are perceived. But that does not imply that the world is the same thing as the data provided by my senses. There is a mismatch between what medicine and neuroscience can tell us about our experience, and what it is like to do that experiencing. For now, we need to focus exclusively on the latter.

In order to respond to what happens around us, our experience needs to be interpreted – good and bad, near and far, threat or opportunity – and that process of interpreting the world introduces the elements of value and meaning that are key to our sense of home, and indeed to almost everything about us. As we locate ourselves within the world, we start to sense where we are and whether or not we are 'at home'.

THE DEN

Children love making dens in a wood. Just a few branches locked together and covered with smaller brushwood will do. They have created a space that is theirs. They sit inside, looking out on to the untamed nature around them. They have a home and, returning to the same wood several weeks later, may be saddened to see that their den has fallen into disrepair, with perhaps little to show for it other than a pile of branches strewn about.

As a child, I made a den in a shed at the back of our house, and surrounded myself with my most treasured belongings. It was my personal space, to which others could only be admitted with my permission. And even before that, in play, I constructed my personal space under the dining table, separated off from the rest of the world by draped sheets. I would crawl under there, look out on to the outside world of the room, and feel comfortably enclosed in my own little house. Later, my space was a spot at the bottom of the garden, to which I would retreat from time to time and in which I would suddenly feel 'at home' in a way that I did not understand. All I knew, was that I wanted to be there.

Growing up, I started to feel at home in school and made new friends who shared that home. In my teenage years, with a social life located in the nearby town, I felt deprived by living out in a village, isolated six miles from the land of promise. My earlier circles had started to be overlaid with others, broader, more specific, more socially defined.

At college, friendships were forged with people from all over, our common bond, our shared 'home' being the subject we studied, the experience of singing together in a choir, or living together in a student hostel. More circles; more identities to be laid over the earlier ones.

And through that process, seen particularly starkly in the years of adolescence and young adulthood, comes the insistent and problematic self-questioning: Who am I? Where do I belong? The circles of personal space are no longer simply geographical or physically concentric, but interlocking and of different strengths. Growing up is the process of under-standing and setting relative values to those circles.

MAPPING

The process of discovering significant places and people gradually builds into our map of our world. And like the oldest maps, it is illustrated with attractions and warnings, with places that matter, where we feel 'at home', and places where we sense we are lost, or to which we feel no particular attachment.

46

We grow into our map. There is no hidden or mysterious 'self', it is simply the product of the on-going interaction we have had with our environment and what we have made of it. The mind plots out our world in space and time, investing it with meaning, providing orientation and giving us a sense of identity.

Memory is the other essential component of this process; loss of memory is loss of self. The person with memory loss knows 'how to' but forgets content, and therefore progressively fails to function socially. Without memory, we don't know who we are, nor the way to get 'home' from where we are, for it is memory that stores the templates that enable us to interpret our experience. They shape our emotional health. As Freud pointed out, patterns laid down in childhood may return to haunt and warp our adult experience.

Sometimes the memory is conscious, as when we are reminded of an earlier event; sometimes our new experience comes laden with dread, or sadness, or excitement, and we cannot understand why it does so. We may be comfortable, superficially well provided for, and yet lost. We may even forget the home for which we unconsciously long. We may have neglected the ambition that earlier shaped our map, leaving us with no more than a general feeling of unease, disorientation or of time that has been wasted.

But still we move around the internal map of our world, like a spider in a web, affected by every vibration and change.

We started this chapter with Proust, so let us return to him at this point. He ends the first volume of *In Search of Lost Time* by saying:

> The places that we have known belong now only to the little world of space on which we map them for our own convenience. None of them was ever more than a thin slice, held between the contiguous impressions that composed our life at that time; remembrance of a

particular form is but regret for a particular moment; and houses, roads, avenues are as fugitive, alas, as the years.

Exactly so; our maps trace out the fugitive moments that have shaped us. His experience of a madeleine, dipped in tea, reminding him, many years later, of his mother offering it to him, stands at the head of this chapter. What Proust shows, as his remembering unfolds, is that our early maps remain with us, haunting and enriching our lives, giving them shape.

Our maps interlock with those of others. When a friend or relative dies, they leave a gap in our lives, a space on our personal map that they are no longer there to fill. Or rather, their space changes into one that presents us with no more than memories. But we too have a place on the maps of everyone we know and, as our significance in their life changes as time passes, our coordinates on their maps shift. One day, we will be no more, and our place on their maps will be represented only by the memories they have of us.

The maps offered by social or commercial transactions can easily lead to isolation and loneliness; a sense of not mattering, of not having a place where we are recognised, known and valued. Loneliness is also disorientation, a sense that our supporting map has gone.

Consciously or unconsciously, we are constantly writing stories and making maps. They tell us who we are and where we belong. They shape both our self-understanding and our understanding of others; they influence how we respond to the challenges of life and our relationships with other people.

When it becomes conscious, making maps gives us a visual way to sort out our priorities, reflecting on what is central and what is peripheral. It is engaged philosophy – thinking about our world as active participants, not just observers.

LOOK UP!

Look up from this book and just be aware for a moment of what is around you. Chances are that, if you feel comfortable in your surroundings, almost all of what you see – whether people, furniture, other books, photographs, a garden – will have a particular meaning for you. Imagine it as a three-dimensional map opening up before you. You get up and move, and the map changes in front of you. It is as though you have a radar system that picks out things of significance as they come within the range of your senses.

If you're travelling, it will be the same. The car may be your own, perhaps identified with dropped sweet wrappers and the other detritus of family life. If pristine, it still proclaims the make of car you chose for yourself. Even if it's a rental car, it still represents something in your personal map – the way you've organised a journey from one place of significance to another. Your journey is all about where you're going, and what that means within your life.

My camera has a 'face tracking' facility. As soon as a human face appears in the viewfinder, it is noted and encased in a little yellow square. Every human face is identified in the same way, and I am free to decide which face I want to have in sharp focus by toggling from one to another. That selection of who is to be in focus gives the image its character and shows the intention of the photographer.

I suggest that the same process takes place, quite unconsciously, as we engage with the world. Nourished and made sensitive by remembered experience, we are constantly selecting the relative importance of features in the world around us, sifting out elements within our personal space to find the things that speak of home and give emotional comfort.

So look around: What does all this mean to you? What does being here at this moment represent for you? Are you 'at home' in a conventional sense? What is it that makes you feel emotionally comfortable or uncomfortable? Or are you reading this book to kill time because you are somewhere you don't want to be? If so, what does even *that* say about you?

Step forward into your map and, like the area picked out by the headlights as you drive down an unlit road, new points of significance and meaning come into view. Shut your eyes and you can imagine yourself elsewhere, but that imagined place will also be mapped with significance.

The living room of the late Jan van Borssum Buisman, artist, sculptor and former curator of the Teylers Museum in Haarlem, Holland. Aspects of his life are reflected in the objects with which he surrounded himself. However, an important feature of his map is not on display, for he was a secret agent in World War II. Do we all have elements in our map that we choose not to display?

There are two processes happening here. On a physical level, your senses are exploring the world and conveying information to your brain, but that information is then processed and located; it is mapped. You do not just see things, but locate them and give them significance. Without

50

that second process, your world would be, literally, meaningless – the sad fate of those who suffer from advanced dementia.

THE SIX DIMENSIONS OF MAPPING

Maps need not be flat, static or unambiguous. Thinking of the world of our experience as a map, requires it to have six dimensions:

- With only two dimensions it would be no more than a flat image, into which we would not venture, a continuously changing *trompe d'oeil*, giving only the illusion of depth.

- With three dimensions it becomes a 1:1 scale representation of the world in which we find ourselves, but we remain detached observers, and what we see remains meaningless.

- With four dimensions, time is added to create a narrative. This is the level at which we engage with stage and screen, imaginatively entering into a world that has been created for our amusement or edification. We may enjoy consuming maps that are created at this level, but only once the sixth dimension has been added, as we shall see.

- A fifth dimension is complexity. You can engage at different levels with this kind of map. It offers physical space and time into which you can enter and move around, but it also offers a blending of different layers, each reflecting a different aspect of life. Families, careers, relationships and responsibilities are mapped out here. The map changes according to the priorities we have at any one moment; it enables us to be creative and see things differently. But at this point we remain passive; the map simply presents us with potential benefits or threats.

- Until, that is, we add the sixth dimension and find that the map also responds to our touch – physical, emotional or intellectual, solitary or shared. The six-dimensional world, mapped before us, now invites, or demands, personal engagement. It becomes plastic, we can change it and take responsibility for it; we can decide whether to get involved or stand back. Some parts of the world invite us to make choices, others are remote, too large, seemingly beyond the influence of any individual. But this six dimensional map has become the experience of a living individual and, amazingly, it is what consciousness provides for us at every waking moment.

The last two dimensions of the map are crucial. Finding our place in a static world is simply a matter of 'fitting in', but with those last two dimensions the map becomes interactive. As we engage with it, we impress upon it our values and preferences and discover that it moulds itself to accommodate them. This opens up the dimension of ethical choice.

In the world examined by science, everything appears to be determined by pre-existing causes. We need not get diverted here by the debate about whether that is a feature of the world itself or merely of our way of understanding it. Whichever is the case, the world appears inflexible and completely determined. Seen in those terms, we have no choice, no responsibility and no hope; science or fate render us impotent.

But that's not how we experience the world. Although we know that our freedom is not absolute, we still find that we can still make a difference. We have choices to make and consequences with which to live. The world's experienced plasticity is a mid-point between physical determinism and absolute freedom. Our maps are not fixed; we can shape them.

THERAPY AND EMOTION

In his book *The Sane Society*, Eric Fromm[12] suggests that five things are needed for mental health:

1) Relatedness
2) Transcendence/creativeness
3) Rootness – feeling at home
4) Identity/individuality
5) Orientation/devotion – finding something worth living for.

This present book argues that numbers three, four and five are closely related to one another and spring from a sense of belonging, having a 'home' of some sort. They form the basis of identity, by giving life purpose and direction – essentially, what Fromm thinks of as devotion. Therefore, if we consciously engage with the process of mapping, it has the potential to become a form of personal therapy.

Personal mapping is intuited. As I travel across the country, I hit 'warm' patches – perhaps places I have lived at some stage in life, or where friends live. Equally, I pass through cool patches, which may be physically delightful, comfortable, wealthy and offering everything that I might normally see as desirable, but which are devoid of any personal significance for me. My world is intuitively plotted out over the physical terrain.

On reflection, my life and thought has been shaped by the quest for home. Partly, this is physical: Where do I belong? At which points on this globe do I feel at home? Partly it is intellectual: I sense that I am 'at home' among people who think in ways similar to my own, or share my values. There is an element of personal history too: I am at home among circles of friends whom I have known for a long time. Even after years of separation, meeting old friends offers a comforting sense of acceptance. They belong to an earlier map, and therefore have a place in my life. I engage with them initially using the earlier coordinates, but may now have the opportunity to up-date and re-locate them on my map.

53

But home is not just an inner experience to be cultivated – although it is certainly at least that – but also something external to be discovered. I need to *be* at home, as well as to *feel* at home. My question, therefore – fundamental here – is this: can we find and enjoy an internal sense of home without any external correspondence? Can we, of our own making, create our inner purpose without reference to some overall sense of meaning? More to the point, can we – without loss of integrity – seriously commit to an internal experience if it appears to fly in the face of external facts? To put it crudely, are visionaries and positive thinkers pissing into the wind? That's what cynics among us might suggest. Are they right?

To address this, we need to reflect on the various experiences of home that have shaped us as we travel through life. It might help to take some blank sheets of paper, and on each try to draw a diagram of our values, hopes and fears at each stage of our life. Set them alongside one another and survey them – they show your mapping, but do so in terms of real experiences and situations. This actually happened; this is how I felt; this is when my life changed. There is no magic or psychological trick involved; this is simply a way of reflecting on your life, mapping it out and learning from it.

One of the most famous of all spiritual and intellectual recommendations, used by Nietzsche in *Thus Spoke Zarathustra*, but found back in the fifth century BCE in the work of the Greek poet Pindar, advises, 'become who you are'. Finding integrity is key to adulthood. But in terms of personal space, that advice is transposed. It is now a matter of: 'live at home, wherever that is for you. If you move, take that sense of home with you. If you choose to live as a stranger in any place, beware the danger of also becoming a stranger to yourself'.

It is a truism to say that we are shaped by our early relationships. Mother and father, siblings and first friends – through all of them we are testing out who we are and how we might achieve happiness, comfort, solidarity, a sense of purpose and direction. Failure at the early stages of this process can warp for life.

In order for children to grow to maturity, they need to learn that they are not the centre of the world, but have their place in a network of relationships. That requires an important refinement to our process of mapmaking. Points of significance for us – whether a person, a place or an idea – have a place in other people's maps, and exist also in their own right. Our personal map *interprets*; it does not *define*. If we assume that our relationship with another person *defines* them – in other words, they have significance only by being on our particular map – then we are in deep trouble.

Our own mapping interacts naturally with that of others. Let me give you a simple, almost casual example of such an interaction, along with the process of mapping as we engage with somewhere new.

JAPAN ...

'Welcome to Shinkanzen Hikari bound for Okayama.' I am surprised and relieved to find that announcements are relayed in both Japanese and English. The landscape is slipping by at 160 miles an hour; the train's raised track and silence adding to the sense of unreality, detached from the urban sprawl below. I sit with a can of Asahi and a packet of crackers; shoes off, swishing south-westwards from Tokyo.

An astonishing landscape, familiar to me only from Japanese art, flashes past. Flat stretches of land, completely over-developed – house roofs, tiny gardens, open paddy fields tucked between industrial zones; everything flows below us as we glide on. The paddy fields are becoming bright green with their new crop of rice; a heron stands motionless, watching for life in the water. There are wires everywhere, haphazard, strung like a crazy net along the streets. Suburban roofs, their lower parts turned upwards like pagodas. Then into a wooded, steep-sided mountain, the darkness of the tunnel for a moment, before emerging again above the flatland. Places of simplicity; places of the kami; shrines clinging to the slopes; silence above the bustle of the streets below.

The businessman on the seat opposite becomes agitated. He looks up at me and at my camera, then out of the window, until he can contain himself no longer. 'Fuji san' he blurts out, leaning forward and gesturing out of the window. And there it is, off to the right, the perfect cone of Mount Fuji, made starker on the skyline by its snowy summit. It is his special place, a key feature of his map, and he is afraid that this tourist will miss it. I nod my thanks, 'Aragato', and raise my camera. He smiles at my attempted Japanese; indulges me; silently welcoming me to part of his world; introducing me to an aspect of his map.

And yet, in this unfamiliar landscape, I am starting to feel at home. Perhaps it is the fact that I'm staying with my daughter in Kurashiki, and her presence adds a special layer of meaning to my visit. Perhaps also that I see everywhere tokens of my interest in Buddhism, images and shrines bringing alive what previously was experienced in practice and books.

I stand at a shrine on the other side of the world, pay respects to the Buddha *rupa*, and suddenly I am at home. There is a depth here that speaks to me. For a moment I sense that I would be happy to die here; that I belong here. Yet how can this be, in a far distant land? Where does this come from? The spirit of place touches ideas long ingested, expresses before my eyes the objects of my reflection and reading. I have never been to this place before, and yet it is a homecoming, a recognition of a part of myself never before located in quite this way.

In Kyoto I find myself facing the famous sand-garden; I notice how the roofs of the shrine blend exactly into the folds of the landscape. I sit quietly on the boarded walkway; something is sinking into me, like a comfortable mist. My heart warms, expands; I feel tears welling up. Let this stay forever. Why did

I waste all those years? Why the stupidity and foolish decisions of my personal history? Why have I not recognised this before? And yet here ... This I could always have been, as I fit myself, like a grain of raked sand, into the wider flow of life.

At Nara, walking slowly through the park towards the shrine with the enormous Buddha, I watch the deer and the carp, and suddenly they embody what is taught in meditation: the delicate walking of the one; the smooth flexing of the other. I see them here and feel them inwardly; they speak of something that is me, or that I aspire to grow within me.

But notice the layers of experience here. My sensation is bound up with deeper convictions, this time about Buddhist ideas, but also a sense of quiet – harking back perhaps to the silence of the riverbank near my childhood home. Here, in my later years, a childhood home re-asserts itself on the other side of the world.

At this moment, to the internalised question 'who am I?' I would not even consider an answer in terms of neuroscience, or my physical body, or even the basic definition in terms of nationality and place of residence. Who I am at this point is deeper and more meaningful; this is the better self to which I aspire. This is a sense of belonging and identity that contrasts with so much superficiality. In this moment of bursting emotion, I also sense the guilt and loss of so much un-lived life, of times and choices that did not reflect this better identity.

Here, in this landscape, I catch glimpses of who I aspire to be; I sense myself 'at home' in this foreign land. What is visible here mirrors my inner experience. The map of meaning that it presents to my senses is congruent with others long established, reinforces them and affirms continuity. I rest in this personal space; sink into it; feel utterly comfortable. I am at home.

IS MAPMAKING HEALTHY?

Is mapmaking healthy? One might as well ask whether breathing is healthy. We may breathe in poisonous gas and suffer as a result, we may gasp fresh air and feel rejuvenated, we may breathe slowly to relax, or quicken the breath to compensate for the burning of oxygen as we increase our activity. We can't help breathing. The question is, do we appreciate how we are breathing? Can we benefit from controlling the breath?

I would suggest that the process of mapmaking can be good or bad, creative or destructive, mind-expanding or mind-constricting. Of course, like so many features of life, it can become distorted; psychopathology examines where personal maps go wrong. But that possibility should not blind us to the benefits of being aware of our ever-growing map. It is the fundamental orientation we take, the process by which the world becomes personal and takes on value. It is what makes us human, separates us from machines, gives us an emotional life that feels worthwhile. It is 'yes saying'; it is affirmation; it is the defiant rejection of a determinism that imposes impotence upon us, however rational and scientific that may appear.

Objectively, we may be no more than dust on the surface of an insignificant planet, but that is not the scale of our interaction with the world. We need to explore our meaning through the choices we make and the places we call home. If Nietzsche is right and the horizon has gone, if there is no more up or down to this life, we can either become cynical and despairing, or we can pick up the pieces and set out to define our own horizon.

In this chapter we have explored the process I call 'mapping'. It happens naturally and continuously, and gives us a value-rich and nuanced view of our world. It expresses our hopes and fears as well as carrying along our past into our present. In a world that would otherwise be impersonal, it creates our 'personal space' and in particular it gives us a sense of home.

Our maps do more than set out our personal world; they show what we have become. They do not *illustrate* our story; they *are* our story.

But what does this say about the mind–body complex that makes us a human being? Within the philosophy of mind, thinkers tend to be divided between materialists and dualists, with the balance between the two approaches swinging one way and then the other with changing intellectual fashion. By the end of the twentieth century, it seemed that materialism – backed by discoveries in neuroscience – would dominate thinking about the human mind and its relationship to the body. But then, as so often happens, the limitations of the materialist view have caused some to examine again the older dualist tradition, presented in philosophical terms from Plato to Descartes, and maintained throughout in western religions, where a mind, self or soul is separate from the physical body.

How we understand ourselves reflects how we understand our world, and vice versa. As we discover our home, we also discover ourselves. But how might that process relate to what is happening in our brain?

Today, any account of how we experience the world needs to relate to the world of neuroscience, if it is to be credible. Therefore, we need to pause and consider what is going on behind our eyes and how that impacts on our sense of personal identity.

'My formula for happiness: a Yes, a No, a straight line, a goal.'
Friedrich Nietzsche

When it comes to shaping landscape and personal space, the Dutch excel. Nietzsche would surely have approved of the Afsluitdijk, cutting out across the sea, straight as a die.

Chapter 3

Behind my Eyes

For most of us ... the habit of locating consciousness in
the head is so ingrained that it is difficult to think otherwise.

Julian Jaynes[13]

Behind my eyes are the bony sockets in my skull and the soft
greyness of my brain, but that is not at all what I experience.
As I open my eyes it is as though a window opens up before
me, and I – located behind my eyes – look out into the world
through a wide space stretching almost from ear to ear. I
know that, in medical or scientific terms – my act of seeing is
no more than a chemical and electrical process going on
between eyes and brain, but that's not how it feels. The eye
sockets sit either side of the place where I have the sense of
'me'. That is the point from which my perspective on the
world originates. And what is more, as I look at you, I assume
that you are also hidden in your head, with your personality
revealed particularly through your eyes – windows into your
soul. As you turn towards me, I sense a communication being
established with something quite other than the physical
contents of your skull.

Any physical process has its limitations. My perception of the
world may be distorted by defective eyesight, giddiness,
alcohol or psychedelic drugs. I know that what I see depends

61

to that extent on how well my senses work, but I would be unable to function if I genuinely believed that what I assume I encounter as the external world were no more than a product of my senses and brain. Dreams and hallucinations may replicate that experience, but do not thereby deny its reality and, if I cannot tell the difference, I'm in deep trouble.

Vague or clear, precise or defective, it is the world that I see, not the process of seeing. I have a point from which I view the world, and need the orientation it affords in order to find my way around, to survive, to escape, to feed or to reproduce.

What happens behind my eyes makes my world unique and gives me a sense of who I am. Although affected by hormones, a chemical imbalance, blood sugar levels or other physical features, one thing is certain – my experiencing must be related to my brain, because that is the centre of operations, both physically and experientially. It is sometimes claimed that a perfect neuroscience would give a total description of who we are. That may, or may not be the case, but what is indubitable is that any feature as broad and universal as I have suggested the process of mapping to be, should find some correlate in neural activity.

To be credible, therefore, the process of mapping, described in the previous chapter in terms of personal experience, needs to be related to brain activity as revealed by neuroscience. What we seek, without getting into technical details, is some correlation between the neural and the experiential.

It is important to find that, because otherwise we could give in to an all-too-easy separation between what we experience on a personal level and what we know through science. I cannot conceive of myself as merely a collection of neurones firing within my skull, and yet I cannot deny that, in a physical sense, my brain is in charge of a process that makes me possible.

TAXI!

Following the Great Exhibition in London's Hyde Park in 1851, there were complaints from visitors that the drivers of their horse-drawn carriages didn't know their way around. As a result, it was agreed that all London cabbies should be required to memorise street names, so that they could navigate without consulting maps. With the passing of years and the expansion of London, this required those who wanted to be licensed to drive a black cab to spend many hours pottering around on a scooter, with a map pinned to their handlebars, memorising 25,000 streets, along with public buildings, theatres, restaurants and railway stations within six miles of Charing Cross. Today, even with the help of technology, gaining 'the knowledge', remains a daunting task. It is unsurprising therefore to find that the right posterior hippocampus of London cabbies – the part of the brain that deals with spatial orientation – tends to be enlarged.

That extreme and oft-quoted example points to a significant feature of map-making and other aspects of our mental life, namely that regular use enhances our abilities. What starts off requiring serious concentration and mental effort becomes easier with practice, and may eventually become automatic. Do you remember your first driving lesson? Or, more embarrassing, your first venture on to the dance floor?

The fact that the hippocampus is involved in our sense of direction and orientation does not invalidate the act of learning to find our way around London. What happens behind our eyes is not some scientifically validated *alternative* to our experience of our world, it simply describes the mechanism by which it is achieved. The actions of turning right, changing gear or launching into a quickstep may eventually be put into effect effortlessly by the brain, but that is only because experience of those things has shaped and streamlined its operation.

The relationship between our brain and our experiencing, as we engage with the rest of the world, is clearly iterative. To claim otherwise is to endorse one of the most implausible theories about the relationship between mind and body – epiphenomenalism. This is the idea that the mind is simply a by-product of brain activity. That makes no sense. Our awareness of personal space and of home comes about because we remember where we have been and what we have felt. Those memories then inform subsequent experience, but although they may be stored in the brain, they are not *caused* by it. The material that forms our personal maps comes from our engagement with the world, not from within our skulls.

That is not to deny that the brain gives a helping hand with that process. Based on our memory of everything that has happened to us, our brain naturally sifts experience for elements of meaning, purpose and causality, as well as the more immediate needs for food, shelter and sex. In that sense, the process of mapping is hard-wired rather than taught. It is what we do and have always done, and without it we could not survive. My experience provides the *content* of my world; but my evolving brain takes, interprets and stores it.

Except in the case of serious malfunction or degeneration, you are not the result of your brain activity; that activity is the result of your living and experiencing the world in which you are embedded. When Buddhists and others speak of training the mind to be more aware of our responses and emotions, their techniques have a measurable effect. Meditation techniques can indeed train us to become calmer or more alert. But any resulting change in neural activity is no different in principle from the increase in size of the London cabbie's hippocampus. Would-be cabbies are not selected on the basis of hippocampus size; they just become that way.

COGNITIVE FRAMEWORKS

Experience and memory build up cognitive frameworks, which are then used to interpret the world and to maintain a sense of self. This process starts with the small child, and continues through life, although, as the frameworks become long established, they become less pliable.

We have spoken mainly of maps, because they seem to be the nearest analogy we have to the way the patterning of value and meaning appears in our day-to-day experience. We see things of value 'out there' in the world, and orientate ourselves accordingly. But the same process can be described in terms of cognitive frameworks – the patterns of ideas and values that are used for interpretation and understanding our world. These, in turn, may be expressed physically in terms of neural pathways, etched by experience upon the brain.

In other words, behind my eyes, my brain is constantly shaping and re-shaping its neural pathways, which record the 'maps' of my past experience and therefore guide the way in which I subsequently interpret the world. This process of cognitive mapping supports decision-making, since it uses information about places, beliefs, meanings and things remembered. Psychology shows both the need for, and the mechanism by which, the process of mapping takes place.[14]

From the point of view of neuroscience, our ability to sense where we are may indeed be located in the hippocampus, but that's not how it is experienced, any more than a journey by car is experienced in terms of the firing of cylinders or turning of wheels. What neuroscience shows is the physical correlation between our experience and brain activity.

I want to argue that the process of finding our way around and knowing where we are, can be described as taking place on three levels:

1) At the neural level, we have measurable activity in the hippocampus that corresponds to our experience, our orientation and our response to the world around us.

2) At the intellectual level, cognitive mapping can be used as a technique in education, planning and management.

We can set out our ideas and relate them to one another through diagrams. At the simplest level, when trying to work out a problem, I take a blank sheet of paper and scrawl bubbles and arrows all over it, each representing an aspect of the problem and its relationship to all other aspects of my life and the universe! I keep looking at the patterns that emerge within the diagram, adjusting the arrows, scribbling things out and moving them around. One sheet is discarded and another takes its place; the map is being refined until it 'makes sense' to me. I suggest that the reason such mind-mapping can work for us, is precisely because it copies the fundamental process by which we ordinarily engage with the world.

3) On the experiential level the senses provide data that we sift and evaluate and which then finds its place on our mental map. If an experience is painful, we learn to avoid it in the future; if attractive, it shapes our future desires. I don't need to have that blank sheet of paper in front of me; I am living within my map and it is being constantly revised. By the time we become adults, some of its features are likely to remain largely unchanged – they are what makes us who we are – but more superficial elements wax and wane, shaping our development.

Our sense of self thus develops in an iterative process with the maps that interpret our world. I remember good times and bad. Pride and shame infuse my memories; I regret times wasted, opportunities lost; I resolve to act differently in the future. It is as though, through memory, I am browsing a novel about my life that I have written spontaneously with little thought given to plot or character development. I am shaped by my unfolding story, which is constantly updated to reflect who I feel myself to be.

The breakdown of this mapping process is seen in the tragic, degenerative effects of Alzheimer's disease, the dying of neurones and dendrites leads the brain to lose the richness of

66

these cognitive frameworks, and thus to revert to a simple experience of the present. Without access to our developing maps, we lose our orientation and awareness of 'home', depriving us of a sense of self. It is a terrible thing to witness, in someone we know; the moments of confused or frightened blankness that reveal the loss of self that personal mapping had previously provided.

THE CONNECTED HEMISPHERES

Neuroscience reveals the physical matrix of our consciousness, but what it can't show – however elaborate and precise it may become – is *what it is like* to experience something. This is what philosophers tend to refer to as the 'hard problem' of consciousness – the gulf that exists between observing mental activity and actually being engaged in it.

We therefore need to be very cautious before we assume that pain, pleasure and the hippocampus can fully explain our experienced world. Descartes famously thought that the pineal gland was the link between thought and physical matter, and therefore the seat of the soul. He was later shown to be wrong, but his quest to find a specific point at which ideas and thoughts in the mind make a physical difference remains a constant temptation. However, it is more likely that many different parts of the brain are involved in any one mental operation, so we cannot simply put a tick beside the hippocampus as providing our sense of home. Something far more sophisticated is happening behind our eyes.

It would be as unrealistic to argue that any one part of the brain is exclusively responsible for our longings for direction and home, as to claim that our leg muscles are responsible for the delight we may take from a walk in the countryside. But, if we insist on finding a place where our development of personal space finds a physical correlate, the hippocampus is as good a starting point as any, which is why it has been introduced into our argument.

Fortunately, to cultivate a sense of home, we do not need to understand neuroscience, except that, from time to time, theories about the brain can illuminate how we see the world. In this context, I want to mention two books, without attempting to do justice to their arguments.

The older of the two is by Julian Jaynes (1920–97), an American psychologist who, for many years, researched consciousness at the universities of Yale and Princeton. In *The Origin of Consciousness in the Breakdown of the Bicameral Mind* (1976) he examines the different functioning of the right and left sides of the brain and links it to changes in the way we view and describe the world. The key feature of his argument is that, about 3,000 years ago, the way in which people understood themselves changed. Prior to that, people did not display consciousness as we now recognise it; rather, they had intuitions of the gods speaking to them, intuitions that originated in the residual speech areas in the right side of the brain. With the coming of society in the form of cities and trade, this 'bicameral' arrangement gave way to the sense of individual choice and intention – the birth of what we now know as consciousness. I would take issue with some of his arguments, but that is beyond our present study. All we need to note, in our exploration of personal space, is that he argues that the right hemisphere of the brain establishes spatial connections and creativity, but that its function has changed. In the modern world, the inner voice that presents our intuitions is seen as part of our conscious mind, whereas at the earlier stage, such voices were thought of as coming from the gods. This, of course, has huge implications both for our understanding of the function of religion and for our understanding of human consciousness.

The relationship between the two sides of the brain has been given a far broader interpretation by Ian McGilchrist (1953–) formerly an Oxford academic and consultant psychiatrist, who writes and lectures internationally. In his hugely impressive book *The Master and his Emissary* (2009, 2019) he seeks to get beyond the 'myth' of the distinction between the operation of the right and left sides of the brain, by examining the different ways in which each contributes to the functioning of the mind, and by acknowledging that both sides are involved in our mental operations. The 'myth' that he dispels was that the left side of the brain dealt exclusively with rationality and language, whilst the right was concerned with intuition and orientation – reflecting a clash, almost, between the scientific and the cultural.

But, most importantly, part of the 'myth' had been that the right side of the brain was involved with fantasy, as opposed to the left, which dealt with science and the facts about the world around us. And that, of course, would be one interpretation of Jaynes' work, since he sees the right side as contributing to the words of the gods, directing life prior to the development of human consciousness. The point that McGilchrist makes, which is essential to our present study, is that the right side contributes significantly by balancing the left. What it deals with is part of the real world, even if it is expressed in terms that are more related to personal and cultural spheres. It is certainly not fantasy, even if its contribution is not set out in logical and mathematical terms.

His argument reflects two quotations from Kant's *Critique of Pure Reason*, which encapsulate the need for a balance between concepts and intuitions, and thus the two hemispheres of the brain:

> Concepts without intuitions are empty; intuitions without concepts are blind.

and

> The understanding cannot see, the senses cannot think. By their union only can knowledge be produced.[15]

Such a view is also reflected in this quote from Einstein:

> Science without religion is lame, religion without science is blind.[16]

The implications of Einstein's quote are open to debate, but one thing of crucial significance for our argument comes from these quotes. Our engagement with, and appreciation of the world cannot be simple and unambiguous. It certainly cannot be reduced to the firing of neurones or the stimulation of our senses; it is a complex involving the interplay of senses, reason, values, memory and intuitions that may well be beyond the reach of our conscious thought. When we speak of personal space, or of home, we are not engaging in fantasy or speculation; we are integrating complementary but essential components of our experience.

The fact that the brain has two connected hemispheres allows it to achieve a balance, where the right hemisphere takes a general view and expressed values, while the left does more detailed analysis. The key problem, as McGilchrist present it, is that, in modern society, the left hemisphere, which was originally there to do the work allocated by the right, has now usurped the right's position. In other words, the Emissary (left hemisphere) is trying to do the work of the Master (right hemisphere). Hence the danger that we might assume that scientific and rational analysis alone, coming from the left hemisphere, will provide a picture of the world capable of solving problems of value and meaning. For a balanced view, we need *both* sides to do their respective work, joined by the hundreds of millions of fibres in the corpus callosum, the neural tissue sitting at the base of the two hemispheres and connecting them.

Enough of neuroscience! It has come into our argument in order to establish one thing only: what happens in the brain may correspond to our mapping and sense of self. What it cannot do is *generate* it. For that we need an external world with which to engage, giving rise to our experiences, which in turn shape our personality, our perspective on the world and our home.

70

WHO AM I?

'I was born under a wand'rin star' growled Lee Marvin, in the much-watched clip from the film *Paint Your Wagon*, which went on to become an unusual hit in the UK pop charts in March 1970. We get the image of the man packing his mules and riding out, an independent-minded drifter, always different, slightly threatening, unpredictable, lawless.

When such men ride into town, the conservative and domesticated folk wince and prepare to defend themselves, hoping that, if they don't soon move on, the wild men will settle down, adopt somewhere as home, fit in with its expectations, grow beans. But the quest for home is not an invitation to conform, and if the wild man or woman settles down, something of their character will inevitably be lost.

It's not easy to give an honest answer to the question 'who are you?' Can anything I say about myself not be coloured by my own wishes and delusions? Are my motives inevitably hidden, so that my best intentions are merely a cover for what is more shameful or selfish? Or am I a 'soul' in need of salvation, and thus at the mercy of the doctrines of religion? Or do I follow Marx, or capitalism, and understand myself primarily in class or economic terms? Am I defined by my attraction to the images I browse in the colour supplement, my history of on-line shopping, or by the ideas of those who march with me carrying banners?

To answer the question 'who are you?' I need to reflect on where I belong, which places attract me and which repel.

As all targeted advertising demonstrates, I am already pigeonholed in terms of my age and interests, where I live, my level of disposable income, my previous purchases, my subscriptions, the newspapers I buy (or don't buy) and my on-line search history. These things say who I am, because they all suggest circles of interest with which I identify. They are the trace I leave behind as I move through life; tokens of my engagement. They are who I am, but not how I may be

71

defined. They show the post-facto circles of my life, and I will certainly change over time; there is no option to remain static.

We therefore understand ourselves best in terms of the spaces we inhabit, whether physical, cultural, emotional or mental. We imagine what it would be like to be married, or have a different job, or to be retired – we have images of ourselves surrounded by different fixtures and fittings, economic, practical, relational. We envisage the personal space into which we want to move, the door through which we want to pass.

No two people will have exactly the same image of the place they would like to think of as home. For some, a solitary house in wild, open countryside would be ideal; for others it would suggest social isolation and boredom. Our dreams of a future home reflect who we are.

Beware of anyone who does not seem to require some form of personal space – they are either unimaginative or spiritually perfect. To live in the present moment, without clinging to the things that appear to define us, is the ultimate Zen experience. To achieve it we would need to be absolutely focused, clear, uncluttered. Few achieve that state; perhaps those who do so simply carry their personal space with them.

BY THE POOL

Sometimes our sense of identity is bizarre. I have to confess –
if confession is appropriate – that the notes for this section are
being jotted on a spiral notepad (there are times when a
laptop just will not do), sprawled on a sun lounger in the
naturist corner of a hotel on La Palma. It's a modest area – as
befits its occupants – suitably screened from the rest of the
hotel. A small pool, surrounded by decking and sun loungers,
is bordered by shrubs and trees. Away from the crowds, the
only sound here is the trickling of water flowing in and out of
the pool, suddenly enhanced as a human body displaces its
volume into the overflow channels.

Objectively, we appear a sad bunch. All of us are of an age
that suggests we first stripped off in the 1960s or 70s, and are
now in the stage of life when the battle against gravity is lost.
We pad around, comfortable in our own skins, happy to be in
this open, vulnerable state, totally in the environment, with
the touch of air and sun on the body, the sense of being
utterly in nature and totally accepting of ourselves for who
and what we are. No attempt here to preen. Bliss!

And this too offers a sense of home: a shared home, a global
home perhaps. Unless they speak, I have no idea of the
nationality of my fellow naturists, for here nationality is
invisible. Nor, once undressed, can we use any of the little
tokens of social status that clothes convey.

So I find myself, surrounded by other people, mostly senior,
sunning themselves, sleeping, minding their own business,
taking the occasional dip. It is curiously un-cool. Gone is the
sexiness of skimpy clothes designed to distract from bodily
imperfections. Here we face the naked truth. We are a motley
crew, brought together by the simple fact that shedding
clothes is yet another way to be 'at home'. Nakedness defines
a small part of our maps and thus contributes to our identity.
We 'belong' here because of who we are, but being here also
contributes to who we are.

Sadly, just a few days later, the area was closed and taped off, the trickling water silenced and the steps into the pool removed; Spain had gone into its Covid-19 lockdown. The virus now imposed upon us a natural equality that previously we had chosen by going naked.

KNOWING OUR STORY

We reveal ourselves through the stories we tell of our lives, as the UK radio programme *Desert Island Discs* illustrates. By combining autobiographical anecdotes with music chosen to reflect particular times or aspects of the subject's life, the programme allows that person's self-understanding to emerge.

The same thing happens at a funeral. The person giving an oration tries to convey, through anecdotes, a sense of who the deceased was. It is the moment when that person's map is laid out, every story revealing something of his or her personality. And, at the same time, the mourners turn over in their minds their own memories, reflecting on the places he or she held in their own personal maps.

Time, like space, is shaped by special moments, standing out against a background that has long since been forgotten. The best man, at a wedding, relates anecdotes to present a caricature of the bridegroom. Most listeners, especially the new bride, hope it is not the whole story!

Every event leaves its residue on our personality. As I live, I write my own story. That is exactly the challenge of existentialist philosophy, which claims that we do not have a fixed essence to which we have to conform, but give our lives meaning through the conscious choices that we make. We cannot control our circumstances, but we are free to choose what we shall make of them. Integrity is therefore a matter of shaping up a consistent narrative.

We therefore live in either a creative or reactive mode, depending on how we see our story as part of the larger narrative. Circumstances embed it in events over which we have no control – a war, a pandemic, a climate crisis, a famine – and we react against that background. But we can also be creative, making of our personal narrative and space something that is uniquely ours. Subsequently, we interpret our story as best we can; although sometimes it takes the help of a therapist to enable us to grasp its import. In the end, our story is a narrative open to a variety of interpretations, rather than offering a single truth.

We are formed by an intertwined set of stories, reflected in the overlapping circles of our map. We have our family and friends, the place we may call 'home', but also other circles such as our nationality or race, the work we do, the sports or hobbies that form groups within which we operate and find our identity. As we map and re-map our world, we see ourselves in new 'homes' with new identities. We may become nostalgic for the selves we were earlier in life, or we may discount what we have achieved because we long for a future when we may be 'at home' with the elite, the wealthy, the professionally established, or perhaps simply at home with a re-united family.

We may even, whether in despair or quiet resignation, accept death, sensing that it will unite us with those with whom we most want to identify. At other times, our map may fail to connect with our present surroundings, and we end up longing for past or future.

Our stories are not told in isolation. Each intersects with others to become a sub-plot in an on-going narrative.

IDENTITY AND CHANGE

Some years ago, following the death of my father, I moved back into the family home to help my mother readjust to life without him. One evening, soon after my arrival, I went to a meeting of a local society in the village hall. Looking around, some of the people were familiar to me; most were not. But the hall where the meeting was being held had memories for me; it was here, soon after it was built, that I had celebrated my eighteenth birthday.

Over coffee, someone said, "Hello. Are you new to the village?" – not an unreasonable question, since it had been more than twenty years since I left. But, before I could answer, an elderly gentleman intervened. "Of course not" he said, "He's one of us; born in the village. Welcome back!"

I looked around at the assembled company. They were conventionally dressed and, by all appearances, solid Conservative voters. I'd lived away from here, explored radical ideas, flown the family nest to get to university – selecting London simply because it seemed to offer the very opposite of the narrow village life in which I had been brought up. Am I back? Do I really belong here? Have I returned 'home' or simply regressed into the world of my parents?

The conflicting emotions of that moment reflect the multi-layered features of 'home'. During my years away, I had felt at home in the lecture rooms of university and in the world of ideas into which I had plunged. I had been at home with groups of friends who were now scattered around the country and beyond. I belonged, to some extent, to the world of publishing and to the community of writers, via the Society of Authors. I was certainly at home whenever I returned to London. Or was I? Where was my real home? Did I have any number of concentric homes? If so, which formed the hub of that wheel?

I include this personal anecdote, because the question of home is not just one of physical location. Home is broader; home is identity; home is shared experience; home is aspiration and solidarity; home is friendship and shared values. Home is all these things, even when they come into conflict with one another, which is why we need to think about home in order to nurture its positive value. Home is always changing, shifting with our new experiences and how we engage with them.

I do not first understand something and then consider how I will relate to it – whether that 'something' is another person, a political ideology, a book I am reading or a religion – rather, my understanding is informed from the very beginning by the relationship I have with it. I experience it 'as' something; I see and know it only in terms of the existing mental world I inhabit.

Often, it is not the intellectual understanding of a new idea that hits us, but the emotional power of the relationship we have with it. Mapping – whether in concepts, people or places – always has value attached, and a new location on our map may prove exciting and unsettling before we even begin to appreciate its significance.

Back in 1970, Conor Cruise O'Brien (1917–2008), the distinguished Irish academic and politician, gave the T. S. Eliot memorial lectures at the University of Kent. At the time I was a postgraduate theological student at Saint Augustine's College, down the hill in Canterbury, where we were preparing – in my case with a considerable degree of trepidation – for ordination. A group of us piled into a couple of cars and headed up to the university. O'Brien had a reputation for being controversial and challenging, and we were anticipating an intellectual treat.

His lectures, entitled 'The Suspecting Glance', proved to be exactly that. As he spoke on Nietzsche, I listened with a growing sense of excitement. As ordinands, we might have been expected to be wary of Nietzsche, but I found myself mesmerised, grinning from ear to ear. These were ideas of which my parents and sober, religious upbringing would have utterly disapproved. But, as he spoke, I felt myself both challenged and empowered. None of my fellow students appeared to respond in that way, but I found myself attracted to Nietzsche's ideas because they spoke to my longings, reinforced my questions, and seemed to offer a kind of inner stimulation that I found quite irresistible. Fifty years later, I still remember exactly where I was in that auditorium, sitting forward in my seat, only just managing to restrain myself from jumping up and shouting 'Yes!' Had I done so, I'm sure Nietzsche would have approved, but Englishness does not generally encourage such intellectual ejaculations.

Returning to my room at the theological college, I felt utterly out of place. I had found something of a new purpose and direction; I was fired up to rebel against conventional theology. However tenuous my relationship to these new ideas, or my ability to articulate them, I sensed that I now belonged elsewhere. Hearing O'Brien lecture on Nietzsche had placed a new point of significance on my map; one that was to challenge many others, and shift my overall perspective.

Such moments are the exception, but they illustrate the more general process of change. They mark the shifting of identity, which can sometimes feel in equal measure exciting and threatening. With hindsight, I should have stopped to reflect what it was about Nietzsche that had attracted me. As it was, I backed off from doing that intellectual and emotional work, retreating into my existing routine, but with a growing sense of detachment.

This example illustrates an important feature of mapping, namely that what is experienced emotionally may actually point to something rather more conceptual or intellectual that needs to be examined. As it was, I bought a copy of Nietzsche's *Thus Spoke Zarathustra*, stuck it on my bookshelf, and continued to plod on towards ordination. Big mistake! With hindsight, I should have used that opportunity to do some serious thinking and re-evaluation. That is also the benefit of reflecting regularly on our personal space – it gives us the chance to take control of where we are going, and of what we see as our home.

FLATTENING THE IMAGE

From time to time, I design posters for a local society. As I do so, it strikes me that the process of putting the elements of a poster together on screen is remarkably similar to the way in which we understand ourselves in terms of our personal maps.

I start with a background image, which tries to set the tone for the poster, and then add over it, layer by layer, the other images or pieces of text that I want to display. I can adjust their size relevant to one another, and can also decide the level of transparency that each should have. In other words, I can choose to make some things more prominent than others, or add subtle hints without swamping the existing layers.

The result is a multi-layered creation that draws together different aspects into a single image. Each of them means something in itself, but each is enhanced by being part of that overall creation. Viewed from above, this stack of layers reveals the final image. However, before printing it out or putting it online, I 'flatten' it, combining the layers into a single digital image.

Thinking about my identity as a person, I suggest that what I am actually examining is the final 'flattened' image, not the multiple layers. It does not immediately yield its multi-layered origin, or the process by which it has been designed. In real time, only the flattened image is visible; to understand its layers, one needs memory, imagination, intuition or, perhaps, a decent therapist.

The self, looking out through my eyes, is not a separate physical entity, over against my body and its senses. It is not physical; it does not 'exist' in the sense of 'standing out' against other physical entities. It is just the shorthand term we use for the interlocking set of maps that shape who we are.

SO FAR ...

How has our argument developed through these first three chapters?

Having acknowledged the importance of a sense of home, we looked at the existential challenge presented by the impersonal nature of the universe revealed by modern cosmology, taking as our starting point Nietzsche's observation that we have deprived ourselves of a horizon.

To counter this, and to discover how and why we feel at home, we then explored the process of mapping and the way in which cognitive maps shape our experience of the world. The personal, cultural, religious and spiritual aspects of life are mapped over the terrain in which we find ourselves.

Not only does this mapping shape our understanding of the world, it also shows us who we are. We are not simply brains from which the self has emerged as an illusory extra. Our intuitions of home suggest that our relationship with the world is far more complex and interactive than any simple analysis of mind and body might suggest.

Our exploration of personal space has been in response to the threat of an impersonal universe. But, to get Nietzsche's sponge into perspective, we need to go back to a time when the world felt very different.

Chapter 4

Before the Sponge

And the Lord God planted a garden eastward in Eden;
and there he put the man whom he had formed.

Genesis 2:8

If our argument in the previous chapters is correct, the development of personal space and a sense of home is fundamental to human wellbeing and personal identity, while not being incompatible with the findings of neuroscience.

But we still face the mismatch between the world revealed by science and cosmology and the personal world that provides us with a sense of home. If Nietzsche was right, we – humanity as a whole, or at least those who influence our thinking and culture – have taken a sponge and wiped away the horizon. As a result, we are left with a world in which there is no up or down, a world of confusing relativism, constantly threatening us with a loss of meaning and direction and the bleak prospect of nihilism.

So how did the universe look before Nietzsche's sponge? What did it offer that we now lack? How, for example, did the people of earlier ages think of time and space? How did they relate their ideas about the universe to their daily lives?

BEGINNINGS

How far back can we go in our quest for personal space? On the north bank of the Ardeche in central France, a few miles from Vallon-Pont-D'Arc, there is a remarkable cave – La Grotte Chauvet. Here, 35,000 years ago, our ancestors produced the most remarkable art, using wood charcoal. Deep within the cave system, the walls are covered with drawings; herds of horses and bison appear to force themselves towards us out of the rock, their forms moulded round the uneven surface. They are remarkably lifelike in both energy and perspective.

Why? With the daily struggle to survive, why spend hour upon hour deep underground reproducing the animals that roamed the world above? What sort of rituals might have accompanied these animal collages? Did they tell one another stories about these animals? If so, this cave shows the origins of art, narrative and religion.

I suggest that, in creating these images, our ancestors were also creating a special place, somewhere to visit in order to celebrate or at least make sense of their world. Here is a personal space, perhaps also, in a more profound sense, a 'home'; not one to live in, but one to return to, generation after generation, in order to get life into perspective.

No doubt I am projecting modern ideas upon these early people; but that is all any of us can do, because looking this far back we have no direct evidence of the intention behind these amazing drawings.

One thing is certain, however: these are not casual works of art. They are done with devoted attention, and the result is very powerful. Our ancestors entered this cave anticipating something important. But we cannot know what they felt, hoped for or found. That situation changes, however, as we move forward into a world that looks a little more familiar.

For tens of thousands of years, early man had been roaming the earth, spreading out from Africa, colonising and becoming established in new territory, hunting and foraging for food. But as the climate warmed, following the end of the last ice age, about 12,000 years ago, there were fewer mammoths to be hunted and humans started to supplement their diet by gathering and then deliberately cultivating plants. By about 8000 BCE, a new phenomenon had developed in the area of the Middle East known as the Fertile Crescent: agriculture.

With the coming of agriculture, people became more settled and tried to make the land produce sufficient food to allow their numbers to increase without needing to move regularly into new territory. Once they started to settle, the world would have been divided between inhabited space and wilderness, between a mapped and socially structured home and an awesome but unmapped world beyond. The mental map of life was beginning to develop a centre and a periphery.

SYMBOLIC GEOGRAPHY

As agriculture and animal husbandry developed, so people started to build enclosures – places where they could gather their flocks and meet one another. They stored produce, traded and established places of security. Those simple enclosures gradually grew into towns and cities.

Even places referred to by archaeologists as 'cities' were very small. At that time, agriculture was labour intensive, and would therefore have been unable to produce the kind of surplus food that could have sustained an urban population. Nevertheless, a pattern was developing.

Early settlements became the focus and centre of people's lives, organised spaces that contrasted with the world beyond – whether wilderness, desert or sea – which became increasingly threatening, as the survival and hunting skills of their nomadic ancestors were gradually forgotten. And as those early cities developed, we find in them a new and distinctive feature of cultural life: the building of temples and monuments. Then, with the coming of written records, we see what they were thinking. We have the beginnings of religion.

And with religion comes sacred geography. For the ancient Egyptians, for example, each temple claimed to have been built upon the first dry land to emerge out of the primeval waters – in other words, to be the centre of the world, and to have existed in that place since the start of creation. For each of those temples, it implied 'a claim of absolute reality'.[17]

For the literal minded, the fact that each temple claimed the same thing, poses a problem, since they cannot *all* make the same valid claim. That it was not a problem, suggests that the intention was existential, rather than literal or geographical. For the worshipper, each of those temples was celebrated as the centre of his or her world, offering a set of values and principles, embodied in stories of the gods.

For the Egyptians of that time, the East represented the past and the West the future, the dead are buried below, while above is the 'high' status, the abode of the gods. Temples became a way of knowing your position in the world.

Throughout the ancient Near East, the creation of the world starts to be described as the result of the actions of gods, behaving as magnified versions of humans – choosing, speaking, creating – building and shaping a meaningful world.

Key to much of this early cosmology is the idea of a struggle between order and chaos. In Babylonian mythology, it is a battle between Tiamat and Marduk, in which the former is sacrificed and her body divided up to create earth and heaven, establishing the rightful bounds of the inhabited world. Further east, in the Hindu tradition, we have the story of the dismembering of the primal man Purusha, out of whose body are fashioned people of the various castes.

The act of creation brings order out of chaos; a logical and purposeful world out of formless matter.

In the Bible, God moves over the face of the waters and calls everything into being, dividing the waters above from those below, creating between them a firmament and dry land – the world we now inhabit and in which God creates a garden for his newly-created Adam.

Here we are moving from physical imagery towards symbolic, spiritual and existential geography. The philosopher Martin Heidegger makes the link between these horizontal and vertical maps of the ancient world and our present enquiry:

> 'The ultimate source of this spatial imagery of the cosmos ... lies in the biological awareness of space found in man, and shared with many other species, which commonly finds expression in the experience and use of territoriality (later rationalised as a concept). More precisely, it lies in the notion of personal space, in which every degree of social relationship from total intimacy to public distance is set out in culturally determined gradations of distance from the subject'.[18]

Here, a psychological reality is described in geographical terms; the idea of personal space, and therefore of home, starts to shape and define the world.

In the ancient Hebrew tradition, kings were crowned in a temple that represented the mountain at the centre of the world. The far-flung places of the world, in which people find themselves, contrast with their personal commitment to this centre and home. The classic example from the Bible is the point in Isaiah (43:5–6) where, against a background of a people scattered and in exile, it has God proclaiming

> From the sunrise I shall bring your seed
> and from the sunset I shall gather you
> I shall say to the north 'Yield!'
> and to the south: 'Do not withhold!'
> Bring back my sons from a distance
> And my daughters from the end of the earth.

You can almost sense the makings of a film script here – the swelling music as, following disaster, war and separation, the prospect of a happy ending is at last in sight. They are coming back; they will triumph; they are returning home!

Responding to the same situation, the psalmist can grieve that 'by the waters of Babylon we sat down and wept, when we remembered Zion'. Those on the periphery now look back to their true centre, their spiritual 'home' in Jerusalem.

In this way, a new and personal map has been spread over the impersonal terrain of the earth. People are challenged to look to a centre, to belong and to share a single vision. What might have been local commitments are now subsumed under something larger, something global.

This is not an attempt to argue that people of that time believed in some quasi-scientific or objective way that there was an established centre and periphery to the world. That would make no sense, because they had a perfectly good working knowledge of the geography of their areas. No; from the start, this would have been recognised as something symbolic and personal, rather than literal.

In such a cosmology, everything has its place, with the act of creation setting the bounds of sun and moon, the ordering of the seasons, and – in the centre – the place for the chosen of humanity.

Later, Delphi came to be seen as the centre of the Greek world. Tradition has it that the god Zeus sent out two eagles from the ends of the earth, and Delphi was the place where they met.

Within the Roman empire, all roads were said to lead to Rome. On a practical level, they were necessary to hold a disparate empire together. But they represented more than that. They established a physical centre, to which armies could return in triumph.

Roman troops patrolling Hadrian's Wall, in the north of England, must have thought of themselves as holding the bleak northern outposts of an empire and civilisation that stretched back into the warmth of Italy.

Whether we are dealing with space or time, the world was never uniform or isotropic. There were always special places and special times – histories to be narrated, roads to lead back home. Personal maps overlaid the physical terrain, and contradicted one another. Different cultures saw the world differently, each with its own centre. That does not invalidate them; rather it shows that each map was a personal and social construct, a way of making sense of life and of giving unity and purpose to its people.

Alongside this, of course there was another reason to observe and predict the changes to the world. They wanted to understand its patterns, so that they could live in harmony with them. The 12-month solar calendar, with 365 days in the year and the 24 hour day, was devised in ancient Egypt, and Babylonian records from 750 BCE give calculations for predicting eclipses. They believed that the heavens were intimately connected with life on earth. The quest to understand the movements of sun and moon followed their preoccupation with the cycle of life, death and rebirth, and the seasons for planting and harvesting crops.

Religion and philosophy underpinned such observations to present the world as a rational, organised whole. Controlled by forces beyond human control, the world had become a place of personal challenge, of reward or punishment. Ancient cosmology had become psycho-geography.

BACK TO THE FUTURE

The ancient Egyptians related time to space, as we all do when we say we look 'forward' to things, and 'back' on the past. But, unlike us, they regarded the past as being in front of them – something they could see – and the unknown future as being 'behind' them.

They were not alone in this. In Hebrew, the word for 'formerly' is best translated as 'in face'; in other words, in front, and the same is true within ancient Ugaritic culture, as described in the work of Professor Nicolas Wyatt, a specialist in ancient Near Eastern studies, in his book *The Mythic Mind*.[19] The same is true for ancient Greek and for Sanskrit, so the idea of looking forward towards the past is widespread in the ancient world. But what does that do to our understanding of ourselves and our world?

If we stand facing the past, aware of all that has led us to the present moment, we may develop a very conservative attitude, but also one in which we feel we have a known place, a sense of solidarity. We are the product of all we know and see. By contrast, the future, which now lies behind our back, is unknown and potentially threatening.

With that orientation, security comes from what has brought us to this point, not from where we think, or hope, we are going. Our understanding of our place within the scheme of things is rooted, rather than aspirational.

How different things are now. We are relieved that something we once feared is now 'behind' us, and look 'forward' to what will happen next. Our 'map' has shifted through 180 degrees, and with it our world.

We live as though we are driving through life in a car. We look out for what might happen so that we can attempt to avoid it by swerving right or left, if that is what we want to do. Morality, choice and existential challenges are born. Contrast this with the rear-facing view. Fatalism and determinism suggest that our future has already been decided by factors we see as our past is laid out in front of us: this is what life has made me. We are trapped by our history.

In the ancient world, the past legitimises the present. Nicolas Wyatt, observes that:

> It is above all in religious belief and practice, with its hallowing of tradition (the experienced and reconstructed or invented past), and repetition in ritual of established, normative patterns of behaviour, that we discern the formal impact of accumulated cultural experience on a society. The significance of the psychology to which this evidence witnesses is as follows: it is clear that memory of the past is a vital part in the life of a community. It is the past and the perpetuation of its paradigms and values which legitimizes the present. Theology, mythology and ritual are the means whereby this memory is reinforced by constant repetition, and the unknown future can therefore be engaged with confidence. [20]

Ancient Egyptians looked to their past for inspiration and for guidance. It gave them monuments (means of remembering) and rituals. Religion throughout the ancient world was closely related to history; it preserved and re-enacted stories and myths that explained the origins and nature of its societies.

In the old structured universe we are exploring in this chapter, the most people can do is to understand their world and try to go-with-the-flow. By contrast, some modern ideologies –

including capitalism and Marxism – are defined more by the process of change they initiate and the destination they seek: the impossible dream of endless, unhindered growth, or the dictatorship of the proletariat.

The establishment of our orientation is therefore not just an intellectual exercise, or a feature of ancient religions; it is fundamentally about how we see ourselves and look to our future; it is about whether we are to be backward looking or forward looking.

THE SOCIAL IMPACT OF RELIGION

It is a sad feature of western philosophy that it has tended to reduce religion to a set of beliefs and thus to neglect the study of religion as a feature of human life. It may be argued that religions do not generally start with creeds or sets of beliefs, but with the experience of wonder, expressed and shared within communities, leading to the adoption of particular values and socially cohesive patterns of behaviour. Only later, once established, do they tend to formalise their view of the world in terms of beliefs. To put it crudely, the first question to ask of any religion is not 'is it true?' but 'what does it do?' This is illustrated by the development of religion in the ancient Near East, which happened at a time when human numbers were increasing and with it the development of towns and cities.

From the standpoint of the psychology and sociology of religion, it can be argued that, beyond individual religious acts and gestures, there developed, within the newly growing communities and cities, sets of supernatural beliefs and moral or social rules, that had the effect of giving people a sense of belonging to their society, and thus giving it an evolutionary advantage compared with societies that had no such religious beliefs.[21]

But which came first? Which had priority? One argument would be that supernatural beliefs were drafted in to support

90

cultural coherence and group morality. Belief in a god or gods, who would reward the obedient and punish the wicked, can be a convenient way of directing group behaviour. But we might also argue that the beliefs arose naturally, and that – because of them – societies became more integrated and uniform in their moral stance and traditions.

My personal view is that the process was probably cyclic. People gathered together and shared stories and myths, some of which – because they gave a sense of meaning and belonging to the group who heard them – became more established and therefore the basis for ritual actions, formalised beliefs and moral views. The more people felt the benefit of belonging to the circle of those who accepted that particular story, the more they wanted to both defend their beliefs and elaborate on their rituals and moral principles. In the early societies of the Fertile Crescent, the major gods were described as supernatural agents and lawgivers. They legitimised social norms, while at the same time, through the cult and the authority of priests, the establishment legitimised the gods – a very convenient virtuous circle.

In the course of his survey of the sense of space and time in the ancient Near East, Nicolas Wyatt sums up ancient cosmologies in this way:

> It should be clear by now that we are building up a composite picture, with a universe made not just out of 'natural things out there', but of things constructed in the mind by human experience, cerebration and imagination. The world we see and experience is inescapably a world we have created, 'a human world'. Religion is the means by which this world is conceptualized, reified and maintained.[22]

Cultural historians trace this tendency for religion to embed itself in culture. In Mexico, for example, from 4000 BCE there are simple and informal rituals, but over the next millennium they get crafted into distinctive religious forms, and by 2500

BCE there is a state cult, with organised rituals performed by full-time priests. The same process can be traced in Mesopotamia from 5500 BCE, India from 4500 BCE, Pre-dynastic Egypt from 6000 BCE and China from 4500 BCE. Rulers, claiming to have a mandate from heaven, present their power as having the authority of the national god or gods. So, for example, in China, from the start of the bronze age (about 1500 BCE), we see the development of tomb architecture, and public religious ceremonies carried out at great expense. The question remains, however: did the beliefs shape society, or did society shape the beliefs? The gods may give legitimacy to the moral code, but was it the shaping of the moral code – experienced as a need to hold a complex society together – that shaped the stories of the gods?

By the time we arrive at what the philosopher Karl Jaspers called 'the Axial Age', between 800 and 200 BCE, we see the further flourishing of public morality, alongside a newly developing sense of individuality and spirituality – society having moved beyond what Julian Jaynes described as the bicameral mind.

THE SACRED AND THE PROFANE

In his study *The Sacred and the Profane*,[23] Mircea Eliade, a sociologist and historian of religions, argues that both space and time can be understood as either sacred or profane, and we engage with them quite differently. In its profane aspect, space is uniform and flat, measurable by science; in its religious form, space is divided up into special places that have meaning for us.

He sees religion as providing the world with a structure, making it an organised cosmos, and giving significance to human activities. Work, food and sex all have a part to play in the cosmic scheme of things. The problem, as he sees it, is that modern man now lives in a desacralised world, in which the traditional sources of value and direction have been removed. Consequently, feeling the lack of direction, people construct their own limited worlds in order to give their lives meaning. As we shall examine later, these can take the form of political ideals, or more limited interests and activities. In other words, having lost the sense of the world as sacred, we live within the profane, but compensate by building our lives round activities and ideas that appear to give us a sense of belonging and a place in the world.

The contrast between the sacred and the profane is shown in another major shift in human thought and experience: the arrival of philosophy. In Greece, the Pre-Socratic philosophers sought to make sense of their observation of the world, in terms of underlying principles. Thinkers such as Thales and Heraclitus, observed and drew general conclusions, initiating a line of thought that leads to modern science. But, in the east, philosophy had already taken a different approach. Confucius, Lao Tzu and the Buddha were also producing rational systems to explain the world, but for them, the context and aim of their work was to examine the right organisation of society, the quest to become at one with the flow of nature, or the overcoming of human suffering by understanding and training the mind. So – to make a huge generality for the purpose of our argument – in the west, philosophy started to move towards the analytic, empirical and scientific, whereas in the east, it developed in engagement with individual and social need.

There were exceptions, of course, but by and large there developed, from around the sixth century BCE, a divergence between the logical examination of facts, and the engaged, intuitive, cultural exploration of the world. Neither was able to flourish without the other, but their balance influenced the question of whether or not we would ever be able to feel 'at home' in our universe.

This is illustrated by the impact of two of the world's most famous thinkers, one hiding behind the other, Socrates and Plato.

THE CURSE OF SOCRATES

Socrates and Plato have been the subject of vast scholarship and numerous publications, both academic and popular, and I have absolutely nothing to add to that body of literature. I have included them here because I want to argue that, taken together, they were a disaster in terms of our sense of personal space and of home.

Socrates, gadfly of Athens, was famous for his ability to irritate and challenge, and the 'Socratic method' of philosophy, named after him, takes a conventional idea of, say, justice or love, and puts it through a logical interrogation. Common assumptions and intuitions are dismissed in the quest for intellectual precision, ending up with a new definition, that Socrates' intellectually vanquished interlocutors are logically compelled to accept. Now, if clarity is the object of philosophy, then the Socratic method is as good as any. The danger, however, is that it makes logic the principal arbiter of truth. That's fine if you are examining the integrity of statements, but it may not do justice to the added extra meaning conferred through poetry, drama or rhetoric. And it certainly fails as a method of examining the claim that one feels 'at home'. Homes are intuited; they are not defined.

But worse is to follow, and I think the fault now lies squarely with Plato, rather than Socrates. In Plato's famous dialogues, Socrates features as the main protagonist but, as we have no independent evidence about what he thought, we tend to assume that Plato often used him as a mouthpiece for his own views. But whether it was down to Socrates himself or Plato, the damage done by their ideas continues to this day.

For Plato, the individual things we encounter in this world are no more than copies of eternal realities in the archetypal world of the 'Forms'. I may regard a particular thing as beautiful, but only because I somehow have knowledge of the eternal and perfect 'Form' of beauty.

That makes sense in terms of language. The reason I call everything from a Great Dane to a poodle a 'dog' is that I have some notion of what a dog is that transcends the infinite variety of particular dogs. Without such general terms, language as we understand it now would be impossible.

The problem is that Plato applies this principle to the whole range of concepts, so that everything we encounter in the world is a pale reflection of its 'Form'. His eternal pantheon is topped by 'the Form of the Good', knowledge of which enables us to call individual things 'good' and therefore to develop a sense of value and morality.

But notice what has happened here. Reality is no longer seen in the particular things that we encounter with our senses, but in a separate, eternal world. Our life is degraded by being seen as no more than a pale copy of something greater. To make matters worse, Plato argued that he would ban artists from his 'republic', on the grounds that artists produce copies or representation of individual things, which are themselves no more than copies of their Forms, and therefore even further removed from absolute reality. But we might argue that the arts are actually a very good way of conveying emotionally charged intuitions; they express, better than a logical argument, how we actually engage with life.

Why is this a curse? Because it threatens to destroy our maps and sense of home. It points us elsewhere, degrading what we encounter on earth by contrasting it with a perfect, eternal realm, which, for the religious, becomes a 'heaven' to which we go after death.

There is a rather unfair saying – generally used as a criticism of religion – that someone can be 'so heavenly minded that they are of no earthly use'. The same can apply to all dualistic thinking; it degrades present, physical reality. If our 'real' self is not the physical body, we might neglect the latter for the sake of the former. The best of religion has always fought against this tendency, but it is a danger that hovers in the background of much western thought. At its worst, it has allowed torture of the body to save the soul, forcing us to accept 'true' belief for our own eternal good.

When we looked at early cosmology, it was clear that the temple was not necessarily the physical centre of the world, and that the edges were not necessarily marked by the desert or the ocean. That was simply a graphic way to express value and orientation, as was the vertical aspect, with the gods above and the dead below. But look what happens when we match up such ancient maps with the Platonic idea of an ideal world of 'Forms'. What was spiritually 'above' in the sense of giving superior value, now becomes an eternal realm, separate from and in contrast to our present world. In religious terms – and actually, it is not so much religious as philosophical – God has taken his leave as a direct expression of value and creativity, and has disappeared into an eternal realm 'above'. But how can we deny the separate reality of that 'other' realm without at the same time destroying the values to which it pointed? How, in other words, do you take a sponge and wipe away the horizon, without at the same time casting the world adrift, without purpose, meaning or value?

Dualism is the curse of psychological mapmaking, because it suggests that what is of supreme value for us is not at the centre of our map, but beyond all maps.

That, of course, is not the whole story as far as Plato is concerned. In his *Timaeus*, he argues that human morality is based on the order of the cosmos. This hints at what we are exploring, namely that both religion and morality reflect something fundamental – the need to find our way around in the universe, to understand our place within it, and to find our 'home'. Nevertheless, dualism is his legacy in this debate.

ANCIENT VARIETY

Although Plato's contribution was hugely significant, the ancient world was far from uniform in its view.

Aristotle, for example, was in some ways closer to modern science. His 'Natural Law' approach asked about the essence of things and their final cause; in other words their purpose and place within the overall scheme of things.

Then there were the very different views of the Stoics and Epicureans. The Stoics argued that the universe itself was founded on reason, and it was therefore possible both to understand it and to live in harmony with it. This, the Stoics claimed, would bring peace of mind, a sense of purpose, and moral direction. By contrast, Epicurus was an atomist. He considered everything to be made up of atoms in a void, and therefore saw the universe as basically impersonal. In such a world, we need to create personal value and direction by our own choices. Epicureans considered pleasure to be a valid aim of life, but thought that it would best be achieved through moderation and the quiet enjoyment of simple things. In essence, they were arguing that we find our home, our direction and our happiness by choosing to live thoughtfully.

Here, for example is Epicurus' straightforward argument that the universe itself must be infinite...

> Moreover, the universe as a whole is infinite, for whatever is limited has an outermost edge to limit it, and such an edge is defined by something beyond. Since the universe does not have an edge, it has no limit; and since it lacks a limit, it is infinite and unbounded.[24]

Once you have an infinite universe, there is no 'place' for an external controlling agent. Here's Lucretius, a Latin exponent of Epicureanism, knocking away at any superstitious or anthropomorphic interpretation of the world ...

> I will explain by what forces nature steers the courses of the sun and the journeyings of the moon, so that we shall not suppose that they run their yearly races between heaven and earth of their own free will with the amiable intention of promoting the growth of crops and animals,

or that they are rolled round in furtherance of some divine plan.[25]

Notice how different that was from the Stoic view of Marcus Aurelius, who could say …

> Whatever happens has been prepared for you from all eternity. (*Meditations*, 10:5)

The variety in ancient thought is even more striking if you factor in the many different 'Hindu' philosophies from India, the teachings of the Buddha or Mahavira, or further east to encompass Confucius or Lao Tzu. Perhaps, therefore, Nietzsche's sense of novelty in having swept away the horizon, was rather parochial. There had been plenty of earlier thinkers for whom that horizon was never a feature of life.

THE MEDIEVAL WORLD

For most people in the medieval world, however, the horizon was never in doubt. Christianity was presented in dualist terms, contrasting the earthly and the heavenly. It was also underpinned by elements of Greek philosophy as, for example, when the thirteenth century theologian and philosopher Aquinas used Aristotle's ideas in presenting his arguments for the existence of God. But there was a world of difference between the arguments of theologians and the beliefs of ordinary people.

For the medieval mind – whether sophisticated or simple – everything was set within a rational scheme, with God as its guarantor and overseer. Value and purpose, even if it could be established rationally by using Aristotelian logic, was backed by religious authority. Knowing your place within the divine scheme of things was crucial to political and social stability and the only authorised path to spiritual wisdom.

When the medieval person looked up to the stars, set in fixed crystalline spheres, he or she saw meaning and significance, because the Earth was at the centre of the universe, and the life of mankind was the special object of God's concern. Such a purposeful and rational universe protects the human mind against the despair and nihilism of a world where everything may appear to be a product of chance. It offers an external reference, which can give human life a measure of stability and a sense of place. In a medieval context, however, thinking about the world was not separated from religion.

One of the principles adopted by Anselm, Archbishop of Canterbury at the opening of the twelfth century, was *credo ut intelligam* – I believe in order that I may understand – a saying traced back to St Augustine. That phrase, perhaps more than any other, encapsulates Nietzsche's sponge and the shift from the medieval world to the modern. For Anselm, it meant that thinking needed to be done in a context of faith. He wanted to use his reason to explain, to himself as well as to others, what his faith meant. After the rise of science, however, as we shall see, that process was reversed. For David Hume and other philosophers, things should only be believed on sufficient evidence – a view that had earlier been put forward by the Sceptics. The sense of belonging in a providential world, which had been the *starting point* for medieval thinkers, was now a possible, although rather improbable, *conclusion* to a rational examination of evidence. To appreciate the medieval mind, we therefore need to set aside argument for a moment and enter into the emotional experience of its personal space.

Medieval churches and cathedrals create spaces within which rituals are enacted, and around which the community gathers. To enter one of these buildings is to enter a space where symbols point to value and meaning in an otherwise confusing, threatening and uncertain world. Many churches were built facing east, towards the rising sun – in Latin the *oriens* – which enables worshippers to 'orientate' themselves within their world.

We feel it the moment we step into a gothic cathedral. The echo of our footsteps on flagstones, the soaring gothic arches and acres of stained glass, meticulously crafted to draw the eye upwards and through their iconography. Light shafts down across our way as we slowly move up the nave, caressing stone with the colours of glass. We move on, past the pulpit and lectern, under the rood screen and into the chancel. Here the religious world is set out before us. Rows of stalls, each with a heraldic emblem, denoting the status of the person whose seat it is. And then on, up to the high altar, the place of the sacred, elevated, beneath the crucifix, the most challenging of all religious symbols.

Churches, large or small, are mapped out and full of symbolism. Their architectural history and monuments present the personal space of the local community over the centuries.

As I look around, I see a world in miniature. Here Christian values are expressed in stone and glass; an ordered and predictable world. It is one that has hardly changed over the centuries, continuity within a mad world of commercialised obsolescence and ephemeral political causes. What must it have been like, as a medieval monk, to understand the world in these terms?

The medieval system may have been cruel, limiting the ability of the 'lower orders' to better themselves, but that cruelty may have been mitigated by the sense of permanence and 'home' that it engendered. The modern alternative offers individuality and freedom, but without any sense of a timeless certainty. That surely is the existential threat from which a medieval world protected the individual. To be expelled from the familiar brings the threat of wandering the earth with no guiding horizon. Your doom, having shot the albatross, is to sail on forever.

The medieval pilgrim, travelling to a holy place, established it on the map of his or her world. Yet the earthly pilgrimage is but a shallow reflection of a greater one. The 'home' to which one is ultimately travelling is in heaven, to be accessed by death. And this continues to dominate much religious thinking. This earth is a vale of tears, a challenge to faith, a place where one is in training for a greater hereafter. Nowhere on earth will do for a settled home, nowhere deserved an ultimate commitment, always the eyes are to be set on a distant horizon. Jerusalem my happy home … To be a pilgrim … Swing low sweet chariot, coming for to carry me home … My home is over Jordan.

Throughout Christendom, churches were built to a uniform pattern, with an altar representing the holy place, which people could approach to receive sacramental help. Religion helped people to 'know their place' (in both a positive and negative sense) and feel 'at home'. It is difficult to over-estimate the comfort that comes from encountering the familiar in a foreign land. Today, those who follow a religion can enter a place of worship anywhere in the world and feel that they are immediately surrounded by the familiar, by symbols that reflect their values, by a community that shares beliefs, that are held together across other cultural differences by religion. In mosques the mihrab indicate the direction of Mecca, synagogues house the scrolls of the Torah.

The holy became available locally, establishing a place on a globally extended personal map. Here, in this far-flung land, I touch base; I am at home.

The nineteenth century religious thinker Friedrich Schleiermacher famously described religion as the 'sense and taste for the infinite', seeing the universal in the particular and the eternal within the moment. The ordinary, mapped within our familiar terrain, points to something of ultimate value – something to which I can say 'yes' without reservation. Hence, religion was, and for some can still be, one of the ways in which we see our personal space mapped out before us.

SECULAR ALTERNATIVES?

In spite of its inherent problems, Plato's displacement of our home into an intellectual or religious sphere is widespread in popular culture: the dead have been 'called home', leaving the rest of us as pilgrims here on earth.

By contrast, Wittgenstein's later advice to the philosophically inclined was a radical 'don't think; look!' In other words, if you want to know the meaning of a word, look to see how it is being used. Perhaps we should do the same with the Platonic Forms. If you want to know what they are, don't think about whether there can be an eternal realm, or how such Forms might be related to the ordinary things of life, rather take a look at how they are being used.

Essentially, dualists use the idea of Forms as a kind of guide – a set of eternal markers, which stand in contrast to the ephemeral, passing entities with which we have to deal in our everyday life. They provide a set of cosmic values. But how can they apply, if we are now living in a world without an above and below?

We cannot go back. We cannot see the world through the eyes of Plato or pretend to be a medieval monk. The world has moved on. But the question is: what of value has been lost? Can we, in our modern world, recreate what was positive in the ancient sense of 'home'? A fundamental question for us today, whether we are secular or religious, is how to maintain or replace the function played by religion in earlier times.

Perhaps religion needs to disappear in order for people to take responsibility for their 'home' and therefore have no need for some displaced 'home' after death – the sort of argument that Marx was using in the nineteenth century. Or can the function once performed by religion be taken up today in secular form, whether social, political or retail? Is our quest for home a feature of life that can be addressed equally in secular or religious ways? My hunch is the latter.

Consider, for a moment, the implication of this. Along with much else that we have outlined so far, it suggests that the fundamental human need is for cosmology and a sense of home. But in the actual, physical world, that home is ever-changing and vulnerable, threatening a loss of meaning and direction. Religion steps in to attempt to re-create the world in a way that addresses human need. Seen in this way, religion is not an end in itself, but a way of finding and engaging with home, maintaining our personal space in an otherwise impersonal world.

But that's not how people generally think of either personal space or religion today. Personal space is something purely subjective, something we carve out for ourselves, while religion is often reduced to a set of metaphysical propositions, moral rules and a whiff of supernaturalism and mystery. Why has this happened?

When working well, religion is something that Heidegger would call 'ready-to-hand'. It is a tool we can use in order to understand our place in the world and establish ourselves 'at home'. The danger is that we treat it as 'present-at-hand'; in other words, that we examine it as though it were some external part of the world – something 'out there' – rather than a means of dealing with our own human reality. It becomes detached from its natural home-building function and is mistaken for a set of propositions to be accepted or rejected. That reduces both the idea of religion and of personal space to a travesty of their former selves. How has that been possible?

In the next chapter I shall argue that something went terribly wrong. Just as Europe was celebrating the rise of science and the triumph of reason over superstition, it started to lose the plot in terms of personal space.

Even the busiest of places, important as the focus of many people's lives, will eventually fall silent. Two thousand five hundred years ago, this was the town hall of the city of Lato, near Kritsa on the island of Crete.

Chapter 5

A Shipwreck of the Heart?

All nature and its laws lay hid in night
God said: Let Newton Be: and all was light.
Alexander Pope, *Essay on Man,* 1733–4

You know how it is. One moment you are predictably bobbing along on the ocean of life when, suddenly, events overtake you. They may be positive – falling in love, having a child, getting married, entering into some new venture – or negative – illness, divorce, unemployment or bereavement. Waves of change threaten to overwhelm your emotional boat, and you look back in nostalgic despair at just how predictable and safe life seemed before it all happened.

In this chapter I shall argue that, between the fourteenth and the nineteenth centuries, events in Europe created waves that cumulatively swamped the older medieval worldview of personal space and home, causing a shipwreck of the heart and generating the sponge that wiped away Nietzsche's horizon.

It is possible to give only the most hesitant of sketches here, for the complexities of five hundred years of history are far beyond my abilities or the requirements of my argument. But something needs to be said, however inadequately evidenced, because, in the twenty-first century, many people still enjoy

105

studying the philosophy of ancient Greece, cherishing ancient literature, admiring gothic cathedrals, or belonging to one of the world religions – all of which require an imaginative switch from our present way of encountering the world back into that of those earlier times.

Every period of history, in every continent and culture, throws up its particular challenges, so why start with fourteenth century Europe? I have chosen it, because of my experience, year after year, of marking examination scripts on the Philosophy of Religion. One of the regular essay topics requires students to assess the Cosmological Arguments for the existence of God, as set out by the academic and Dominican monk, Thomas Aquinas (1225–74). Using ideas from the newly-discovered works of Aristotle, which had just been translated from the Arabic following years of being lost to the Latin west, Aquinas sought to bring together state-of-the-art philosophy, as it was then, with traditional Christian doctrine. He wanted to support belief in a loving, creator God with sound reason and observation. He described God as the unmoved mover and uncaused cause, underpinning and holding together everything in this fragile and contingent world. What he offered was the ultimate religious vision of a benignly ordered universe – a spiritual 'home' for the believer.

His arguments were exactly right for his time, with the opening up of universities throughout Europe and a sense of intellectual revival, and even today, Aquinas remains *the* theologian for Catholics. However, his arguments no longer represent a philosophical consensus; far from it. His view of the world, and the religious orientation that springs from it, are seen by many philosophers as being of historical interest only – a world long since relegated to the status of human construct, rather than the result of observation and logical deduction.

We can discuss Aquinas today in ways that would have been unthinkable in the thirteenth century, and that has everything to do with our changed perception of the universe, our sense

106

of personal space, and our idea of home. So, in this chapter, I want to explore what has happened since the time of Aquinas.

However, before outlining some waves that have rocked our collective emotional boat over the centuries, we need to admit that our perspective here is parochial. The argument would be quite different if we had scope to consider the work of Confucius, Lao Tzu or the Buddha. Those three great eastern thinkers have a great deal to contribute to our idea of home, but they do not directly answer Nietzsche's challenge, so, unfortunately, we need to bracket out their thought.

It is also clear that there was no single or simple view of the world prior to these events. The worlds of classical Greece and Rome were quite different from those of the Vikings or the ancient Britons, and the religious worlds of Judaism, Christianity and Islam were never fully homogenised in terms of beliefs and practices. But the key thing to keep in mind is that, for all of them, there was a narrative that sought to explain life as a whole and to give the individual a significant place within it. Their maps were different, but at least they were recognisable as maps.

So what happened? In the broadest of terms, I want to suggest here some features of those centuries that might have contributed to Nietzsche's sponge.

HOME DURING AND AFTER A PANDEMIC

We all know now what it is like to live through a global pandemic. While I was writing this book, Covid-19 dominated the news with daily statistics of those infected, hospitalised or killed. The numbers numb. We can hardly open ourselves to the scale of the suffering that lies behind them. The world becomes a dangerous place as we venture out wearing a mask. We celebrate those who, at great risk to themselves, continue to work in the medical and essential services. We feel shock when the virus touches those we know.

Our bereavements are linked to those of all our fellow human beings.

But even in our present situation, it is difficult to appreciate the scale of the horrors brought by the Black Death in the fourteenth century. In the early part of that century, even in the years of war or famine, the basic infrastructure of culture and civilisation seemed well established. Priests, monks and nuns, maintained a network of social as well as spiritual provision, and throughout Europe, the energy that was being poured into the building of parish churches, cathedrals and monasteries, spoke both of religious certainties but also of local loyalty and rivalry. People were literally building their sense of home and of security. This paralleled the local nature of governance; people's lives were largely controlled and justice administered locally, rather than nationally. While history tends to focus on major political events – including the beginning of the Hundred Years' War in the mid-century – for most people in the fourteenth century, the most significant events would have been those that touched them locally.

But during the 1340s, the bubonic plague spread westwards from China towards Europe, arriving in Britain by ship during 1348 and 1349. Spread from person to person, probably through fleas, the Black Death moved, slowly but remorselessly, across the countryside. Deaths from the plague were horrible, and it was widely regarded as divine punishment, adding guilt to physical pain.

The Black Death went on to kill about half the population of Europe; in some cases entire villages were wiped out. In 2020 people commented on the silence at the start of lockdown, as traffic stopped and the skies were empty of planes. Imagine the deeper silence when every inhabitant of a village is dead, and the traveller walks past nothing but empty houses, crops going to waste in the fields and a deserted church. Without the benefit of daily news updates, they would move through a devastated landscape, never knowing what horror they would encounter next or the extent of the disease.

In terms of 'home', it is instructive to observe the initial reaction of government in the aftermath of that pandemic. In England, the authorities attempted to preserve things as they had been before the plague struck, fixing the price of goods and wages, preventing people from leaving their manors to seek work elsewhere, and even forbidding them to eat food or wear dress above their station. But they failed. With such a dramatic drop in population, working people who survived could demand better food and lower rents, and there were urban revolts throughout Europe. People became both more mobile and more materialistic. If the skills they offered were in short supply, they could move on and sell their labour elsewhere. Landlords were threatened with the prospect of being left without tenants or rent. Working people became aware of their worth and responded accordingly, moving to better themselves.

Of course, local control in terms of parish churches, priests, landowners and justices of the peace continued. But I think that something quite fundamental changed with the Black Death. The sense of being rooted in a God-given, fixed place was giving way to something more flexible and more like our modern capitalist society.

If they were discontented with their lot, working people could seek employment elsewhere, taking their personal space with them, seeking to establish a new home. And looking around at empty villages, they would already sense that the old horizons had been wiped away. In England, the Peasants' Revolt of 1381 was sparked by many complaints against landowners and rents, the attempt to restrict upward mobility, along with a call for the end of serfdom. The extent to which the Black Death shaped the society in which these complaints could be made is a matter of debate, and they were hardly new, but it set people asking fundamental questions about life, including questions of loyalty and home.

That said, the century following the arrival of the Black Death showed signs of a determination to mark out personal space and enhance local pride. Newly-generated wealth was channelled into the enlargement and embellishment of perhaps half of all the churches in England. The 'perpendicular' style, with vertical lines emphasising the height of windows, came to dominate the fifteenth century. Although some villages were abandoned after the Black Death, others revived and flourished. Walk around church buildings from this period and you have a sense of a gathered community, where font and altar, baptism, marriage and burial, marked their on-going life.

What should we conclude from that? It would seem that the precariousness of life, even on such a scale, does not detract from the drive to create personal space. If it had, we would never have witnessed the wonderful rebuilding of local churches that took place in the fifteenth century, in spite of a background of almost continuous warfare and heavy taxation. Looking round such buildings one is struck by the idea that the survivors of the Black Death did not give up the quest for personal and social space. An overarching belief in divine providence may have taken a knock as the death toll kept rising, but not the need for a sense of home.

THE CHALLENGING OF RELIGION

Behind the changing features of our day-to-day life, believers – then and now – accept the idea of an eternal and unchanging realm. God reigned supreme, and earthly powers received their own authority from him.

With the Reformation, in the sixteenth century, however, the impact of religion on the sense of place became more problematic. Luther and the other Reformers challenged the authority of the Pope and the Catholic Church, replacing them with the authority of the scriptures and – within limits – the right of individuals to interpret them to the best of their own abilities. In Europe, Protestant and Catholic nations fought one another, with terrible loss of life, and minorities on both sides were persecuted. For individuals, their fate often depended on the willingness to compromise their beliefs when circumstances demanded it.

Prior to the Reformation, religious, moral and intellectual life had largely been based on the authority of the Church, and the unquestioned deference to the philosophy of Aristotle. Belief was not a matter of individual choice, but of dutiful acceptance. The Reformation challenged not just the Church but the whole structure of society and authority.

It would be naïve to claim that Protestants were free to believe what they wanted. With the wars of religion, Protestants and Catholics confronted one another as rival authoritarian political and religious entities, and the Protestant side was quick to start to splinter into different groups, as interpretations of scripture differed.

Nevertheless, the Reformation and the wars of religion that followed it, reinforced an age-old truth, that there could be fundamental disagreements in matters of religion, for which people were prepared to die and to kill. The upheavals in the name of religion were surely another nail in the coffin of belief in a single, divinely organised and ordered world. Personal choice and commitment had taken centre stage. If religion can be challenged and changed, it becomes something for which we are responsible, and thus another feature of the fixed horizon is wiped away.

A WORLD TRANSFORMED

The rise of science, the seventeenth and eighteenth centuries, heralded an age of optimism for forward-thinking people. Reason, evidence and experiment were seen to yield practical benefits and a reliable way to understand the world. Nowhere was this shift more evident than in cosmology.

The radical change in understanding the universe had started a century earlier in the work of a Polish priest and astronomer, Copernicus (1473–1543). The radical nature of his thinking and the boldness of his conclusions were

111

astonishing. After millennia of believing that the Earth was providentially set at the centre of the universe, surrounded by glassy spheres, as set out by the Alexandrian scientist and mathematician Ptolemy (c100–c170), he observed, calculated and declared that the Earth revolved around the sun once every year, while rotating every day. Also, having observed that there was no shift in the relative positions of the stars when viewed from different places on Earth, he concluded that they must be considerably further away from the Earth than was the sun. His book *De Revolutionibus Orbium* dealt a devastating blow to the traditional view of the universe.

The potential conflict with religious authority was mitigated by the addition of a preface by the Lutheran theologian Osiander, who suggested that Copernicus had merely provided a more convenient model for thinking about the workings of the universe, while not denying that, in reality, it was as described in the Scriptures. That attempt to mask its impact did not last, and by the time Copernicus' work was developed by Galileo (1564–1642), the conflict between observation and authority was unavoidable. The map of the universe was being re-drawn, on the basis of observation and calculation.

Modern cosmology is based on mathematical physics; it develops formulae and makes testable predictions. It is highly abstract and far removed from the experience of the world provided by the senses. In addition, its findings have a degree of certainty that – in our present state of knowledge – appear compelling. So, for example, the Big Bang theory of the origin of the universe was confirmed in 1965 by the discovery of the microwave background radiation that had been predicted by the Big Bang theory and therefore turned it from a possibility – set over against the 'steady state' theory – into the 'standard model' of the universe. Of course, one day that model will be revised or replaced – that is the very essence of progress in scientific knowledge – but, for now, it would take a considerable amount of contrary evidence to bring that about.

It is not easy, therefore, to see how there can be a meaningful dialogue between cosmology and traditional religious view of the world. They appear to come from totally different spheres. One of the issues is whether the world is finite or infinite. The logic of traditional theology is that only a finite world is compatible with the idea of a creator God, since an infinite one has nowhere to locate an external or prior creator. That has led some religious thinkers to welcome the Big Bang as it leaves open a prior activity of God, whereas the 'steady state' theory would have made God redundant. But are such attempts to relate theology and cosmology worthwhile? Back in 1956, the Christian theologian Eric Mascall, whose views were generally regarded as conservative and carefully balanced, said 'The whole question whether the world has a beginning or not is, in the last resort, profoundly unimportant for theology'.[26]

The implication of this would seem to be that, however precise and logically sound the scientific understanding of the universe may be, it does not, in itself, either disprove or endorse a broadly religious viewpoint. But of course, that is dependent upon the religious viewpoint not attempting to claim scientific validity. Religious and personal views are essentially existential, and should be appreciated as such.

This fundamental shift in cosmology, however unimportant for theology, is absolutely relevant to our sense of home. It shifts us straight back to the 'Brooklyn' problem. What has the new way of understanding the universe done to our sense of home?

THE THEORY OF KNOWLEDGE

In parallel with the shift in cosmology, there was an equally radical change in the theory of knowledge. Francis Bacon (1561–1626) opposed Aristotle's idea of 'final causes'; in other words that everything happened for a purpose or to fulfil its essential nature, and based all knowledge on evidence. He set out rules for assessing it, warning against the danger of accepting only what confirms that which we wish to be true. That view was developed by the philosopher John Locke (1632–1704), who set out principles for establishing human knowledge, based on the observations and the application of reason. He distinguished between primary qualities, such as physical extension, and secondary qualities of colour, smell and taste; the former existing 'out there' in nature, the latter produced by the operation of our senses. The developing sciences were concerned with the former, and tended to bracket out the latter. Determined to get an objective view, rather than a subjective one, it came to see the real as the measurable. Everything was there to be counted. Our experiences could be 'reduced' to physical reality – the colour of the rose to a particular wavelength of light impacting on my retina; the music to the frequencies causing movements picked up by my ears. In this way, science was revealing a world that was explicable and logical, but devoid of the richness of human experience; a world of the head, but not of the heart.

A similar thing happened with the use of statistics in the early nineteenth century. Until then, every event was treated as a particular and distinct occurrence, although reflecting general laws or principles. The fact that there might be many other similar occurrences did not detract from its significance. But with the use of statistical measurement, each event loses its uniqueness. It is now explained in terms of statistical probability, a realm with its own laws and explanations. Statistics are fine until they are used to explain our own behaviour or views. Then we start to protest that we act from our own free choice, not due to some invisible hand of the markets or statistics.

But, to return to the seventeenth century, we see that, with Bacon and Locke, the principles upon which evidence should be assessed provided a necessary basis upon which scientific method could operate. Nothing should be accepted on the grounds of authority alone, nor simply because we may wish it to be so, but only after careful observation and thought.

Locke claimed that the mind starts as a blank sheet, a *tabula rasa*; everything we know comes from experience. Such knowledge is always open to be revised as our experience grows. Our horizon is not fixed but grows with us – another element of the sponge falls into place.

The philosopher and scientist who best embodied those changes in understanding the world is Isaac Newton (1642–1727). The title of his greatest work says it all: *The Mathematical Principles of Natural Philosophy*. He developed calculus, and established the principles of mechanics and optics, and did so, not on the basis of established tradition or authority, but on mathematics. The way of thinking about the world had taken an entirely new turn.

The medieval world, following Aristotle, had a tendency to ask 'why?' To understand something was to place it within the overall scheme of things: to comprehend its purpose. Not so for Isaac Newton. He shifted away from that approach in a radical way, famously declared *'hypotheses non fingo'* (I make no hypotheses)[27] ... That may sound improbable, because science is always putting forward hypotheses, but for him it had a particular meaning. He observed, measured and devised theories to enable successful predictions. Having successfully described *the way in which* gravity worked, he did not consider it necessary to try to describe *how* or *why* it worked.

Assuming that nature works in a uniform way, the future can be predicted on the basis of present observation. So, for Newton, it was not essential to know 'why' something was as it was, only 'that' it was. His task was to deduce theories from observations. What he set aside – and called 'hypotheses' – were those things not so deduced. In a stroke, he had rejected the speculative approach of medieval theologians.

This, in itself, transforms the sense of personal space. We do not inhabit a purposeful world designed for our benefit. Things do not happen as an expression of divine purpose, but as a result of measurable causes. The world becomes an intricate machine, within which we find ourselves as intermeshing cogs, determined by the laws of cause and effect. Such a world is inherently impersonal.

From such a perspective, space was a way of describing volumes, surfaces or points remote from one another, mapped out, as on a grid. No one place was any more important or significant than another.

Science thus presents space as impersonal and homogenous, but that is not how we experience it. As we have already seen, space is shaped by our commitments and our emotions. 'Home' is not just a location, but a whole range of emotionally significant experiences. When we are 'lost' the feeling is rather more than is required simply by having mislaid a literal map, or turned off our satellite navigation. Being 'lost' is an emotional state in which our surroundings are strange, unfriendly and potentially hostile. That is the fundamental difference between scientifically examined and quantified space, and space as we experience it.

Whatever existential questions the new world of science may have raised, there can be no doubting its practical benefits. By the end of the eighteenth century, life had been transformed by new technology, including the steam engine, the sextant, the hot air balloon and gas lighting. The industrial revolution was being born. Compared with the sixteenth century, the world at the end of the eighteenth seems remarkably modern, even as its horizon had become rather less distinct, and certainly less fixed. The universe was ruled by laws of nature, discoverable by human reason and put to use in new technology.

The assumption, from that time onwards, was that everything could be measured. With Adam Smith, we see the birth of the science of economics: value and production become measurable. For his friend, the philosopher David Hume, empiricism demands that evidence should be weighed for and against a proposition, and judgement suspended until the evidence points decisively, or at least proportional to the evidence available for and against. Perhaps the most significant new way of thinking, for our purposes, is the idea of utility, used by Jeremy Bentham to judge moral questions. He considered that the right thing to do was whatever would produce the greatest good for the greatest number, weighing benefits according to their intensity, their duration and how immediate they were.

Thus, even morality and conscience, the most personal aspects of our engagement with the world, are to be subject to measurement and calculation. That was not the whole story, as we shall see later, but it changed the parameters of debate, with just a hint that, if it can't be measured, it can't be real. And home, of course, cannot be measured in that way.

COFFEE AND GOOD ARGUMENTS

Although the intellectual ferment of the seventeenth and eighteenth centuries was astonishing, the Enlightenment, or Age of Reason, did not come about against a background of political consensus, peace and general good will. Alas, the opposite was the case. From the regicide, commonwealth and civil war in seventeenth century Britain, through the eighteenth century wars in Europe and on to the American War of Independence and the French Revolution, it was a troubled, bloody and heavily taxed time. Clearly, the intellect had not triumphed over human emotion, ambition or folly.

In spite of that, and in many ways, the Enlightenment, more than any other period, has shaped modern society. Much of what we take for granted today, in terms of political organisation, science, free speech, religious freedom, and the assumption that the human world can and should progress, find their origins in this period. It gave us capitalism, science and democracy, with freedom for individuals to think, speak and to draw their own conclusions. It saw the rise of the coffee house as a place to meet and discuss everything in free and inclusive debate.

The Bible continued to sell more than any other book, but it was also possible, although unusual, to be an atheist – as, for example, was the philosopher David Hume. Social mores could be mocked in novels and human resourcefulness in the face of adversity celebrated, Robinson Crusoe being the classic example – cast alone upon a desert island, he uses his wits to survive and establish himself.

One might assume, therefore, that we should look back on the Enlightenment as a time offering unqualified benefit to humankind. Few would choose to live without science, medicine, democracy, individual rights and the prioritising of reason over prejudice and superstition. But, it was not without its problems, for its rejection of earlier superstition and authority, undermined the way in which many people had thought about themselves, their place in the world and their sense of home. But the changes it brought about were, by intention, creative rather than destructive.

A new sense of intellectual home was also emerging from the debates of that period. People of different classes and backgrounds were increasingly able to meet and discuss on equal terms. Ideas were circulated in newspapers, pamphlets, magazines and books, creating circles of readers bound together by shared ideas. In earlier centuries, with lower levels of literacy, this would have been possible for only a few; now it was thrown open to a larger section of the population, particularly in major cities. New layers of 'home' were being added with every convivial or challenging discussion in London's coffee houses. People were starting to belong to the shared world of ideas and getting a taste for free and honest expression; for many, their world and their sense of personal space was enlarging.

THE ENLIGHTENED INDIVIDUAL

If there is one person who can stand as the embodiment of the European Enlightenment, it is arguably the German philosopher Immanuel Kant (1724–1804), who remains one of the most influential figures in modern philosophy. His work contributed to the theory of knowledge, ethics and aesthetics, and he also took an interest in cosmology. But while his intellectual life explored new realms, his physical life remained remarkably static. He was born, educated, worked and eventually died in Königsberg – then part of Germany, but now in Russia and called Kaliningrad – and the regularity of his daily walks was such that people were said to set their watches by him. His enormous output of original thought was produced alongside teaching commitments at the university. He was well read and prodigiously creative. Yet his prodigious workload did not prevent him from having many friends and being remarkably good company. He seems to have been utterly at home in his own, very clearly defined, personal space.

Inspired, he claimed, by the starry heavens about him and the moral law within him, he created an integrated view of the world, in which he made a clear distinction between how things are in themselves (what he called 'noumena') and how they appear to us (phenomena). He argued that, since all knowledge comes through the senses, we can never know the former, only the latter. On the other hand, when it comes to the experience of ourselves as moral beings, we have direct awareness of the basic, logical principles upon which we judge things to be right or wrong.

The things that inspired Kant, directly impact on our sense of identity and home. Awareness of the dimensions of the universe and, by implication, our place within it, generates a sense of wonder, but also of helplessness in the face of a world that is both impersonal and beyond our control. But Kant is equally aware of the experience we all have as moral beings, acting freely on the basis of personal choice. He sets out three forms of the 'categorical imperative' which form the bedrock of his moral thinking: that you should be prepared for the principle governing your action to become a universal law; that you should treat people as ends in themselves and never as means to your end; that you should act as though you were legislating for a kingdom of free, autonomous individuals.

Notice particularly the last of these. In earlier times, when asked 'who are you?' the answer would probably have been in terms of family and locality, craft guild or religious membership. Each would specify where you belonged in the pecking order of the various social, political and religious spheres. But now, asked 'who are you?', Kant would answer 'I am a free, autonomous individual; a citizen with rights'.

The Enlightenment thus led to an emphasis on the individual, and on morality based on personal choice and responsibility. It was about refusing to conform to external authority and affirming the right of free people to think and decide what is in their own best interest.

It may have promoted science and led to the establishment of democracy, but the attempt to put reason in charge, was not without its problems, and it is certainly the case that for individual thinkers, 'the life of reason does not necessarily lead to a reasonable life'.[28] Even in the eighteenth century, philosophy could be cruelly mocked. On 2 May 1760, a play by the French playwright and satirist Charles Palissot de Montenoy caused an uproar when it opened at the Comédie Française in Paris. Entitled *Les Philosophes*, it portrayed a bunch of philosophers, including thinly disguised versions of Diderot, Alembert and Jean-Jacques Rousseau, setting out to flatter and deceive a rich widow. Arguing that happiness and self-interest should be their sole motivation, they scheme to have one of their number marry the widow's daughter, Rosalie, to gain her dowry, to her dismay and that of her lover. In the end, good sense and love prevail over the calculations of philosophy.

In the name of ideals, individuals were certainly not always given equal status, nor treated as ends rather than means. The French Revolution may have been driven by ideas and ideals, but its arguments were too often settled by the guillotine.

But there is a more fundamental division highlighted by the two sources of Kant's inspiration; two utterly different ways of being in the world – as an observer and as an engaged individual. As an observer, and to any other observer, we become parts of an impersonal machine, totally conditioned by its laws. People cannot see 'me' as I am in myself, only the image of me presented to their senses. By contrast, as an engaged individual, I have intuitions about how I should behave and can take responsibility for my actions. We shall explore this, in the context of twentieth century philosophy, in the next chapter.

The problem is not whether or not the scientific rationalism that emerged at that time is correct. The problem is that the earlier cosmology had answered an existential need; it formed the basis of religion, value and morality. Once these things were made a matter of personal choice, cosmology lost its former importance, leaving a gap in our lives that science cannot fill.

A SLAVE OF THE PASSIONS

The advances in science during the seventeenth and eighteenth centuries may give the impression that it was a period in which reason dominated all other considerations, and therefore that the emotional and religious influences of earlier times – along with the sense of home shaped by them – ceased to apply. In fact, that was far from the case.

David Hume, although ruthlessly empirical in his arguments about what we can know, took a surprisingly different view when it came to the relationship between value judgements (which he termed the passions) and reason.

> We speak not strictly and philosophically when we talk of the combat of passion and of reason. Reason is, and ought only to be the slave of the passions, and can never pretend to any other office than to serve and obey them.
>
> *A Treatise of Human Nature*

In other words, reason's function is to put into effect those things that we intuit to be right and valuable. Thus, for example, his basis of his ethics is quite different from that of Jeremy Bentham, who weighed up potential benefits and harms in order to decide which course of action should be judged right. Hume, by contrast, argues that morality starts with our natural sense of moral obligation and the feeling of repugnance we experience when we see the suffering of others. However rational, he is actually guided by emotion and intuitions, allowing reason to step in to make a case for what he already believes to be right.

The same would be true of that other great figure of the Scottish Enlightenment, Adam Smith. The one theory most people associate with Smith is the 'invisible hand' by which market forces operate; the guiding principle of liberal economics. But, although that idea appears in his best-known book *The Wealth of Nations*, it does not replace the key thrust of his earlier work *The Theory of Moral Sentiments*. Like Hume, Smith starts with the idea that people want to be thought well of, and therefore seek to achieve that end in the best possible way. His economics is driven by human needs and values, not by an economic algorithm. So, even as the new approach to knowledge and science was gaining ground, it is far from true to claim that the Enlightenment reduced all life to calculation and measurement.

We only have to reflect on the literature, music and art of that period, to realise that the advances in science and the prevailing sense of reason, is only a small part of the overall human story. And that is even more obviously the case if we move on into the nineteenth century.

THE ROMANTIC RESURGENCE

Based on reason alone, the heart dies. That is true of any perspective, whether in the eighteenth century or the twenty-first, based exclusively on measurement, logic, data and statistics, and it was the implications of such a perspective that

Nietzsche described as the cold breath of empty space. Nihilism stalks any perspective that suggests that values can be reduced to a cash equivalent.

The alternative approach – and one that has been taken over the centuries by the creative artist, writer and musician – is to seek to express the feelings and thought that shape our lives, to set them down and see if some coherent story can be told about them. My life craves some sort of narrative shape.

The Romantic Movement of the nineteenth century provided a counterblast to any narrowly empirical perspective, with elegant formality giving way to the attempt to express raw emotion. We feel it in the way in which the wonderful precision of Mozart, gives way to the emotional power of Beethoven. We see it in the intensity of Wordsworth or Blake, the nostalgic longing beneath the surface of Constable's paintings or Hardy's novels, the richness of perception of the Impressionists and so many others.

And all this in a century that also saw the industrial revolution and the publication of Darwin's *On the Origin of Species*. It was a century of remarkable cultural intensity and change. I am bemused by the thought that Charles Darwin on the *Beagle*, heading out on the voyage that was to provide evidence for his theory of natural selection, took as his on-board reading Milton's *Paradise Lost*. His own work was to change people's view about how species come to be, and thus inspired many to see life as an upward progress – from ape to superman, to use Nietzsche's image – whereas Milton explores the very opposite, as human nature stands self-excluded from a physical paradise but with the promise of establishing a paradise within. The one seeks a home shaped by a natural process; the other grieves for a home that has been lost and looks towards a personal replacement.

In theology, you have thinkers such as Friedrich Schleiermacher (1768–1834), who defended religious belief against its cultural despisers, claiming that it offered a 'sense and taste for the infinite', thereby placing it at the heart of a quest to regain and celebrate the richness of life, or the intensity of Søren Kierkegaard (1813–55) whose challenge to decision and commitment paved the way for existentialism. The religious intensity of the period was reflected in Wordsworth's poem *Tintern Abbey* , where he speaks of feeling 'a presence that disturbs me with the joy/Of elevated thoughts ...' Bursting out of any logical argument about whether God exists, it locates the religious impulse in the sense of wonder.

In terms of the quest for personal space and a sense of home, the romantic agenda was set at the end of the eighteenth century by Baron Georg Philipp Friedrich von Hardenberg (1772–1801), better known as the poet Novalis. He was determined to romanticise the world; to see the commonplace as remarkable and to give colour to the drabness of uniformity.

Like many romantics, he was in rebellion against any attempt by science or empiricism to dominate human experience. He sensed that something had been lost, and wanted to reinstate 'home' for a world in danger of becoming homeless.

> Philosophy is really homesickness: the urge to be at home everywhere.
>
> Novalis

The quest for an authentic home environment is reflected also in Blake, whose 'dark Satanic mills' deface the green and pleasant land. Here, in *Jerusalem*, a rich mixture of symbols of home express commitment to the building of a new Jerusalem, giving value and significance to the threatened land.

To me, there is no better expression of the longing for a sense of a home, rooted in apparent security of a long-lost past, than nineteenth century gothic revival in architecture, particularly in the work of Augustus Pugin (1812–52). Best known for designing the interior of the Palace of Westminster, and the

124

clock tower housing Big Ben, he was passionately committed to the gothic revival. The richness of his work in Westminster strives for a sense of history, rooting it in an age of certainty, but it is not the sort of architecture that necessarily shapes our sense of home. For that you need to look at his impact on domestic architecture, for his genius was to initiate a Copernican revolution in house design.

Whereas Georgian architecture had been inspired by classical balance and elegance, Pugin's approach to domestic architecture was pragmatic. He set rooms alongside one another as best suited their use, allowing them to shape the external walls of the house, rather than being constrained by symmetry.

Notice, as you drive through any suburban area, two very different approaches to house design. Some, inspired by the Georgian, are mainly rectangular, formal, with a central door, probably beneath a portico. Others deliberately avoid having a flat front, perhaps by having a bay window extending outwards a front room that itself extends well to the fore of the doorway. Rooms at the back of such a house will almost certainly not end in the same place, but will stretch out – dining room leading through into the kitchen and out into a utility room. Alongside them an open space lets light further into the building. The house has become a collection of rooms working together, rather than a fixed space with rooms set out in uniform rows. We take that approach for granted now, as we extend our house sideways to re-purpose the garage, add a conservatory on the back or put a dormer into the roof. We are creating rooms that will re-shape the house. But much of the inspiration for that came from Pugin, whose own house in Ramsgate in Kent was the embodiment of this new approach, although filled with a richness of ornamentation and wallpaper that most would today find intimidating. The trend was not exclusive to Pugin. William Morris's famous Red House in South London, exhibits the same approach to both the shape and interior design. Both inspired the Arts and

Crafts movement, with its rich, romantic, gothic approach to interior design.

Tea and crumpets at Pugin's fireside? Perhaps a little too rich for some.

So what does this say about home and about our personal space? Pugin sought a link with the medieval and gothic, embodying a sense of eternal values, chivalry and honour. He wanted to surround himself with things that expressed his image of that world – whether that was a historically correct image of that period is, of course, quite another matter. For him, it conveyed a nostalgic longing for an era unsullied by the business and industry of Victorian England.

Don't be fooled, by his romantic notions, into thinking him a dreamer with an easy life. Augustus Pugin was a driven man – a perfectionist and a workaholic. He was married three times, had a large family and died at the age of forty.

A FUNDAMENTAL ISSUE

In this chapter we have explored the idea that the rise of science and the Enlightenment transformed our thinking, giving us freedom of thought and democracy, but also initiated the tendency to see everything as measurable. But, equally, it is clear that philosophers, writers, artists and musicians were never confined to any such mechanical and

126

numerically defined world. During that period, and particularly moving on into the nineteenth century, the richness of human experience continued to be displayed and celebrated.

The result, moving into the twentieth century, was a major intellectual divide, expressed philosophically by two extremes:

On the one hand, following the early work of Wittgenstein, the Logical Positivists, a group of philosophers based in Vienna and inspired by the clarity of scientific language, claimed that statements could only be considered meaningful if they could be backed up by evidence. They therefore dismissed morality, aesthetics, religion and much else in life from the sphere of the 'real' and left them to languish in a world of subjectivity, untethered from the world of empirical knowledge.

On the other hand, the existentialists focused on individual responsibility and choice. As a human being, you do not have a fixed essence, but shape yourself by the choices you make. This was expressed most succinctly by Simone de Beauvoir's famous quote 'One is not born, but rather becomes a woman'. The logical conclusion of that approach is that subjectivity is truth, for subjectivity shapes our world. You are what you make of yourself.

Unfortunately, once questions of morality and meaning are untethered from empirical science and rational investigation, we find ourselves confronted by a postmodern, 'anything goes' approach, in which the individual has a right to state his or her own truth, even if that conflicts with the truth as seen by everyone else. There is no fixed up or down in the postmodern age, and we end up with the nonsense of 'fake news', where there is little regard for conventional ideas about what is true or false, or the findings of science.

Of course, what I present here is no more than a caricature of a whole range of positions that can be argued persuasively. But the point remains that we have come to live in two very different worlds simultaneously. One world, examined by science, is presented in terms of evidence and statistics; the other is the subjective world of value and meaning, in which everyone is free to define and pursue his or her goals.

For the social, moral and political health of humanity, it is desperately important that we achieve a proper balance between the findings of science, mediated largely by the left hemisphere of the brain, and the operations of the right hemisphere in considering matters of value and meaning.

That is why an understanding of personal space and of the idea of home is of such crucial importance, for it is the litmus test of that balance. In what sort of world can we, do we, feel at home?

Chapter 6

Making Homes and Moving On

Where there is no vision, the people perish.
Proverbs 29:18

If a sense of home is essential for our wellbeing, how can we enhance it? How, following trauma, or bereavement, or the breakdown of a relationship, can we start to put ourselves together? How can we have the confidence to move on, or branch out, or enter a new phase of life? Without a sense of 'home' to accompany any of these, we may not literally perish, but we will probably feel that our life is adrift and diminished.

In this chapter we shall take a look at some of the ways in which people strive to establish a sense of home; avoiding the threat of a directionless and meaningless universe. Some develop a passion for gardening or home improvements, or simply re-arrange or de-clutter the place in which they live. Some may commit themselves to a political system, or a career, or a family, or belief in God.

Every situation presents itself as a set of possibilities. At every moment, we have a choice, informed by our personal map and the values expressed through it. Consciously or unconsciously, we refer every thought and every experience to our map in order to give it value and meaning.

Most people only thrive when their world makes sense – to themselves, if to nobody else. For most, there will be a multi-layered pattern of such worlds: family and friends, location, home and garden, the circle of like-minded enthusiasts, a political or cultural world, a career with its peer groups, perhaps also a sense of being part of a global community.

We hope to thrive by establishing a physical home that reflects who we have become, or who we wish to become. Pick up a lifestyle magazine and we are presented with homes designed to reflect the taste (and wealth) of their owners. Look what this person has made of a very ordinary terrace house! Here's how to set your stamp upon a narrowboat, a caravan, an RV with all facilities, a hut in the forest, or a sumptuous penthouse. We look at the images and think: 'Could that be me?' 'Would I want it decorated like that?' Those bookshelves? That open-plan kitchen? The view through the French window and across the patio to the gazebo and pool? Perhaps I am taunted by the fact that the magazine parades a lifestyle that I shall never be able to afford. Is it trying to tell me I'm a failure? However unwisely, we may fall for the intention of the article, and start to wish that we could take ownership of that place, and be 'at home' there. How then would we feel about ourselves? What would we need to be (other than wealthy, of course) to live there? What does it say about us that we aspire to, or simply admire, what it offers?

That glimpse of another possibility for home may contrast with the cramped apartment in which we live, the badly worn furniture, the drabness that we cannot find the will or energy to brighten up. Glimpsing new possibilities may sometimes be cruelly stimulating.

Or perhaps, at the other extreme, the photograph that catches our attention is of a small tent and campfire at night in a wilderness, a comforting pinprick of light in the midst of darkness, the temporary home for the most adventurous. Might that be equally attractive? Could we live in such simplicity for the sake of exploring unknown territory? Or the

130

milder version: the nostalgia evoked by an old Volkswagen camper!

The process, by which we make space our own, works in modest, almost trivial ways. Yet the process itself is far from trivial. It is essential, if we are to feel at home in our world. Deprived of such personal effects, we become dehumanised.

It is Sunday afternoon, and I follow the crowd of personal space-makers into the garden centre. They are on a quest to personalise and improve their environment: garden furniture; patio slabs; shingle; bark chippings; to say nothing of the plants, shrubs and grasses. Such things have their part to play in re-shaping, beautifying and personalising the small portion of the universe to which they claim ownership. Their cars may already be full of paint and other materials from the home improvements store next door. They are designing their own personal worlds – kitchen fitments, floor coverings, colours to choose and compare – encouraged by posters advertising products that suggest a happy family settled in their own space, their ideal home, their environment of happiness.

They are forming their cosmology of house and garden, to express their taste and preferences. They buy living things in pots and place them thoughtfully, in order to place themselves in the wider scheme of things.

Mock none of this; however mundane, it is essential. Just look at what happens when elderly people move out of their own space and into a care home. However kind and attentive the staff, they are always in danger of becoming institutionalised. They try to adapt to their new environment, but, however secure and comfortable, it is not one of their own making, nor one that expresses their personal history. They are in danger of losing features of their former identity, which previously had been reinforced by living within their own personalised space.

So let us look further at just some of the ways in which we find and enhance our personal space and sense of home.

131

THE ESTATE AGENTS' HOME

Located in a desirable area, close to high-performing schools and plenty of green space, preferably within easy commuting distance of a city for purposes of work, shopping and culture. What else should we put on our list? Ah, yes, at least three bedrooms. And the principal bedroom has to have an en suite, unthinkable without. Mock Tudor is not acceptable, I'm afraid, and a classical portico might not be in the best of taste. Nothing showy, but it needs to speak quality.

Fine, if you can afford it. If not, head for the 'compact', 'bijou' and 'cosy'. For the down-at-heel area, try 'charm'; for the dangerous-after-dark, try 'edgy.' Go for the 'rural retreat' to guarantee no facilities within walking – or perhaps even sensible driving – distance.

The art of presenting a house, transforms the factual and utilitarian into the emotionally engaging, creating a nexus of images that give a positive slant to everything that might count against the property. Give it a story; make it a dream. Best, of course, if the sellers can arrange for bread to be baking and coffee brewing during a viewing – there's nothing like the aromas of home to suggest that this box could become one.

We may be tempted to poke fun at the language used by estate agents, but their task is not an easy one. The buyer comes with a notion of the 'home' they seek, an expression of all they want in terms of personal space, which may, or may not, be realistic. What is on offer is something quite different: a utilitarian list, a set of possibilities in a place that – at the moment of first viewing – has no personal resonance. The task of the agent is to intuit the nature of the home being sought, and somehow to shape up the images and hints that will enable to potential buyers to start the process of mapping themselves on to the house he or she plan to sell them.

Identical dreams, piled high?

As a buyer, you visualise yourself in that kitchen, or looking out over that view. You try to imagine the rooms furnished to your own taste.

In other words, you start with an impersonal, built space and location, and try to imagine what it would be like for your points of significance to be mapped upon it. That's where the children would go to school, that's where I could do my local shopping. In viewing a number of potential houses to buy, you find yourself crafting, for each of them, an imaginative reconstruction of what it would be like if one of them were to become your home.

Perhaps the important thing for you is to live somewhere that inspires. Working on your first novel or screenplay? Where would you, as a writer, need to be? London's Hampstead? Paris? LA? A remote hillside? If your map feeds the sense of who you want to be, then choosing the right place might help you to establish yourself. That, at least, is the hope.

Your original family home will never be thought of in this way, because it will already be too heavily laden with

133

memories, good or bad. It may speak of who you were, and perhaps who you want to escape from being.

What is certain, as you scan the advertisements in the estate agent's window, is that you are not looking at a home. You are looking at a piece of impersonal space that, in your view, has the potential to be personalised. You are looking at an empty space on your personal map and wondering whether it could become home. Buyer beware; you are always in danger of trying to buy what is not actually for sale – the self that you want to be once you have that home. Your dream house is, and will probably always remain, exactly that. By contrast, your future 'home' will require effort, personal mapping and the ability to avoid the most obvious hype of the agent's sales pitch.

One final observation, before we despair of finding a chunk of real estate that suits us. Beyond a basic minimum, it's not down to money. Whether you are renting a room, or buying a mansion, the task of making it into a home is not price-dependent. The wealthy are as likely to be emotionally homeless as the poor. By dividing their time between different houses, flitting from continent to continent, their chance of a genuine sense of home and the emotional comfort of personal space is diminished. The more money you have, the more tempted you may be to assume that it can buy you personal space. Big mistake! All it can buy are nicer chunks of *impersonal space*; making it personal requires you to put effort into it – and the wealthy may find themselves too busy to spare the time for that.

HOME ON THE PHONE

There are shortcuts to feeling at home. One of them is the smartphone. The apps that instantly connect you to the rest of your life, testify to the phone's ability to re-create personal space. At any spare moment, you can lift from your pocket the means to check your email, scan the notifications on WhatsApp, dip into one or more of your Facebook groups,

134

respond to comments, Tweet your views, 'like' your friend's latest photo, read whatever news interests you, check on your personal finances, even see whether your car needs refuelling. You pick up the phone to see your life. Indeed, while on the boring commute, the phone may seem to *be* your life. By condensing so much of your life into one place, it becomes your temporary home. Wander into that bleak hotel room, flop on to the bed, and pull out your phone. They are all there – your friends and family, your photographs and videos, your connections or business partners. There may be just time, you realise, to Skype goodnight to your children. However impersonal or temporary your surroundings, you feel comforted. You are tethered, by a long umbilical cord, to the people and places that give you comfort.

Towards the end of 2020, one of the many short videos, which did the rounds to cheer us up during the pandemic, appeared to advertise 'Helping Hands' a spoof organisation whose employees, identified by their 'Helping Hands' T-shirts, are seen gently guiding a person across the street, as he is glued to his phone, or helping to push his child on a swing as he is busy texting. It ends with a man propped up in bed, busy on his phone, while a 'Helping Hand' is next to him in bed, having sex with his partner! Clearly, if you bump into other people while looking at your phone, or find what's on the screen more interesting than what's in your bed, you need a 'Helping Hand'. The truth, of course, is that the phone connects you to so much of your life that the space in which you find yourself physically is not necessarily your true, present location.

Social media provide both advertisements and news on the basis of a feedback loop; that is their power and their danger. Your preferences are analysed, based on your internet use and your responses to previous media events. This then triggers targeted advertising, based on what it assumes you are interested in, thus reinforcing your identity with the products they hope to sell you. In the commercial sphere, belonging is important. I cannot just buy a car, but must now see myself as identified as a 'Toyota family' or with a lifestyle offered by the Mercedes Magazine.

Social media produce strong group identifications because any response is magnified by those feedback loops. You identify and vote because you are the target of media that suggest you are the sort of person who will vote that way. You 'belong' to the brands you support. Your identity is shaped by what you wear, what you drive, where you live, how you vote, your sexual orientation, your race, your religion, your philosophy, and especially your shopping.

I am defined by my cluster of loyalties. Personally, I am a M.A.N. – Mercedes, Apple and Nikon – and if I am approached by another M.A.N., I know we will have much in common: new products to discuss; memories of earlier generations of cars, computers or cameras to share; jargon to keep us in immediate touch with one another, but separated from others present. Two keen amateur photographers, especially if they share the same camera marque, can become happily engrossed in a world of their own. Your purchase of a new 50mm f1.8 lens affirms your status within a group of users, and you can immediately post a photograph of your new acquisition, still in its box, on the appropriate Facebook® group. No, I am not exaggerating; I belong to one such group where, in spite of recommendations to the contrary, people continue to post photographs of boxes!

Targeted advertising works on the basis of the pleasure that comes from enhancing these little interlocking worlds. We may be in the midst of a global pandemic, uncertain about the economic fallout from Brexit or the Trump administration, but I can bask in the comfort of a short video comparing the quality of the f1.8 and f1.2 lenses. My tiny world is controllable and reassuring, it offers a temporary escape from the cold breath of empty space.

Social media enhances our reality, boosting our sense of identity. For some, an event, or meal, or night out is only real once it is posted on Facebook®. Friends – both the real ones and the more distant people who are nevertheless 'friends' by being clicked as such at some point in the past – respond; they 'like', they 'comment', they reinforce the value of what you are doing. Your own personal map now includes their 'likes;' your reality is both physical and media-based.

THE CONSTRUCTED WORLDS OF HOME

What we have been describing here are worlds of our own making. We find meaning in them because we give them meaning. We will them to be the meaning of our earth.

Naturally, we need our own space, perhaps in the form of a room into which we can retreat. This is particularly true of teenagers, who desperately need to mark out their own territory, somewhere they can express themselves and feel secure in the knowledge that their space will not be invaded by adults.

But we also need to make space our own. We plant a flag after having climbed a mountain. We take photographs of places visited – and they become part of our 'owned' space. We discuss places we have visited, compare notes on vacations enjoyed, and as we do so, we add them to our world – our personal 'cosmos'. Some take this further and 'adopt' particular places for their holidays and vacations, visiting them many times a year – a little piece of the world, however far removed from our original home which we seek to adopt. We make it our 'home from home'. In these and many other ways, we take ownership of space, identify with it, and give it emotional value.

This process of personal mapping is found in a range of disciplines. Search in the *Journal of Environmental Psychology* and you will find references to 'place attachment', a feature that is relevant to – among other things – recreational resource management. How you think about managing forests, or designing city centres, is all about creating places to which people will become attached. Places that will register positively on their personal maps.

MIGRATION

Some birds are able to migrate over long distances; they know instinctively how and when to head for home, or for the places where they will breed. Salmon fight their way upstream driven by that urge. Herds of reindeer or bison head south with the first chills of autumn, making for their winter pastures. As the seasons turn, creatures sniff the air, sense change and start to move. They know where they belong at this season. Finding themselves out of place, they start to shift.

Animals mark out their territory and know it intimately. It gives them security. Even for humans, in time of war, local knowledge is invaluable; if you might need to hide at short notice, first make sure you know the best places.

One of the tragic features of modern life is that our natural sense of direction and of home has been eroded. We may move somewhere because we are offered a good mortgage deal, or because of a change of job, or because it is within a reasonable commute of our existing work, or because it is in a zone where housing is affordable. We need have no deep, organic reason for living where we do. We just happen to be there, nothing more. We are no longer able to look at our surroundings, sniff the air, hear the background sounds and know that we are home.

One of the most dubious pieces of advice, given nearly forty years ago by Norman Tebbit, a Conservative politician in the UK, to those who were unemployed, was that they should simply get on their bikes and go in search of work. It highlighted the way in which, in a depersonalised society, people are seen as little more than economic units, to be moved around and used as cogs in the economic wheel. It

138

also highlighted class distinctions. 'On your bike' is hardly the kind of advice to be given to the heir to a great estate, struggling to maintain a property that has been in the family for generations. It is designed for the depersonalised working class.

Whether or not we can maintain our sense of self by migrating, depends on whether the mapped circles of our life are mainly linked to our physical environment. Moving is easier for some than for others, simply because some identify primarily with their work or culture, rather than a particular location. Some choose to migrate in order to flourish. Others have migration forced upon them by an impersonal world, and are obliged to operate in spheres where they are not naturally at home. The ultimate tragedy, of course, is the migration forced by political or economic factors – the refugees who, deprived of their home by conflict or famine, desperately seek a place of security in which to establish themselves. We shall return to the political aspects of home in chapter 8.

THE URBAN HOME

Very little of the earth's surface is urban. It may surprise those whose lives are bound up with cities, but when oceans and mountains, deserts and ice-sheets, forests and grasslands, arable and pastureland are taken into account, only about 1% of this planet is built on. Yet for a majority of people, feeling 'at home' where they live, depends on how that 1% is designed, and their personal history within it.

A small, gathered village, offering the basics of life – healthcare, education, shopping, connections to elsewhere – or the suburban sprawl where individual 'homes' are set out in uniform ranks to the distant horizon. What does each of these say about a sense of belonging? And what of those for whom their urban dwelling is not really the sort of home with which they intended to identify, but a place imposed on their life by work, or the quest to be within the catchment area of a good school, or the limits of their mortgage? What do all these things say about 'home'? Or about how architects and planners set about designing urban areas so that they can become home to those who live in them?

Many years ago, I worked in a new town, where thousands of houses had been set down as a grid over an earlier map of winding lanes and villages. Every now and then, between the uniform rows of houses and neatly ordered streets, a footpath or cycle track would meander off at an angle, the residual marker of an ancient route. And in the midst of this grid stood a thirteenth-century church, tiny and lost, surrounded by mostly untended graves and uncut grass. The building was loved by a handful of elderly residents who had known it as their parish church before the new town came. Their family names were on the memorials, they had been baptised and married there, and generations of their family were resting outside. They would have loved, finally, to have joined them and been buried here, but the site was no longer licensed for burials, so their destiny lay with the local crematorium. But they brought flowers from time to time, and cut the grass round their family plots, and treasured a sense of belonging. The church still had the occasional service, in spite of the attempts to have it closed. It was argued that the worshipping community would be more united if services were limited to a modern building, a mile or so away, devoid of all aesthetic value, character or history. Spirituality had been planned and organised, licensed and set near the shopping centre. But the elderly residents knew otherwise, and clung to their spiritual home.

Walking around that suburban area was a perfect example of maps being laid one over another. To the casual glance, the old village had gone, all bar a couple of farmhouses and the church. On further investigation, signs of the earlier era revealed themselves: names of urban cul-de-sacs reflecting those of long-concreted pastures, or the curious bends in the

140

road, deforming the neat rectangular plan, whispering of long-vanished highways.

Another generation will grow up to regard these suburban wastes as their home, returning perhaps with memories of grandparents' houses and their welcome. The sense of home is generational, and the young families living here now are as likely as not to move on in a few years, as work opportunities present themselves. For them it will have been a good start, a cheap mortgage, a first rung of the housing ladder, an ability to make a bob or two. But was it 'home'? The answer to that lies in the emotional engagement and values of each individual, and the amount of themselves that they invested in this place. Perhaps they came and settled, determined to put down roots; perhaps home was always elsewhere. Who knows?

HAVE WE FORGOTTEN HOW TO DWELL?

In 1951, Martin Heidegger presented a paper entitled *Bauen, Wohnen, Denken (Building, Living, Thinking)*.[29] In exploring the origins of the German word 'Wohnen', which is usually taken to mean simply 'living', he points out that, derived from the word *Wonne*, meaning 'delight', it has the richer meaning of being content, dwelling in peace. In this sense, its context is one of settling to cultivate the earth, to delight in it, cherish and protect it. It becomes genuinely our 'dwelling place'. Even *Bauen* – to build – takes on a deeper meaning, for in the Old High German it meant 'to dwell' and was related to the simple statement *ich bin* – I am – which can therefore also mean 'I dwell'. To be human is to have a dwelling place; to have a home.

Simply having a house does not therefore guarantee that you have a 'dwelling', for the former is simply a means to an end, an opportunity to create a dwelling.

Then, perhaps surprising given the devastation in Germany in the immediate post-war years, Heidegger suggests that the

141

problem people face is not just the immediate one of the housing shortage, but that they have forgotten what it is to 'dwell'. He sees contemporary cosmopolitanism as rootless, and pleads for what amounts to a return to the simply sense of belonging, a sense of home that reflected both one's genetic origins and the place in which one dwells. The example he gives is of a farmhouse in the Black Forest, where a family has lived for generations – exactly his own background.

Belonging to a community and taking part in its celebrations makes a positive contribution to personal space and a sense of home.

Dwelling creates community. Heidegger points out that the original term *Nachgebauer* – near dweller – becomes *Nachbar*, or neighbour. And here the question asked at the end of Jesus' parable of the Good Samaritan is relevant. Asked 'who is my neighbour?' the reply comes 'the one who showed him mercy'. In other words, neighbours are not simply 'near dwellers' but also those who care for one another, who establish the bonds of community.

Heidegger's reflections suggest that 'dwelling' is not simply a matter of filling identical houses on an estate, each the private castle for those who can afford the appropriate level of mortgage. It is marking out a place where people dwell together; where together they forge a home.

MEMORY AND WALKING

When we fall in love with someone, or feel suddenly 'at home' in a place, we learn about ourselves. Something in our own past is evoked – something resonates and causes us, quite unconsciously, to feel elated. The classic example of this process is found in the writings of Marcel Proust, as we saw earlier. Throughout *In Search of Lost Time*, he uses his memory of places and things to evoke the rich tapestry of life. Just the taste of the cake, as he bites into a madeleine, evokes a memory from his childhood, and he is immediately off in his quest to understand and appreciate both the past and the present.

Our memory is a landscape within which we move, always suggesting homes that we have known, perhaps loved, mostly lost. It gives depth and value to the present, helps us remember what we like and what we once hoped for. This does not require a conscious attempt to remember, but is natural and spontaneous. It is the moment when our history wells up to enable us to engage with the present and give it context. I am not a machine, responding to stimuli, but a person with a history, a set of maps, and a sense of where I belong.

Movement, particularly walking, helps reflection. As we walk, so our thoughts clarify, even if it is simply a matter of pacing to and fro in a room. Movement is about purpose and goal, progress and direction. It can also provide an opportunity to slow down, taking time to look around, to become acquainted with our surroundings, to adopt previously unknown territory.

Nietzsche once said 'All truly great thoughts are conceived while walking'. His Zarathustra left his home and went into the mountains to gain his insight, before returning to proclaim his vision. For those able to do so, Nietzsche also suggests one should climb; thoughts are stimulated by the clear air of the mountains.

We need places where we can be ourselves, enriched by our surroundings, whether they come to us through movement or memory. I watch the excitement of the small child, who, taking her first steps, discovers that she can move from room to room. Movement is the freedom to re-position our maps and re-establish our points of interest.

HOME FROM HOME

A few years ago, I wrote *The Philosopher's Beach Book*, a set of short reflections for those on vacation and relaxing on a beach.[30] In it, I distinguished between four types of people on vacation:

- *Explorers* set out to see something new, wander as far as they can afford and are always tempted to go native on food, drink, music and dress. Fundamentally, they are pioneers with ABTA-bonded safety nets.

- *Hedonist-invalids* seek rest and recreation to recover from the stresses of work or the monotony of retirement. They may accept a little cultural input, but are mainly there to enjoy themselves. Cruise liners were full of them, before the coronavirus put the brakes on such hedonism. Younger hedonists reverse the recovery process by partying and ending up the worse for wear.

- *Merchant adventurers* plunder souvenirs and experiences to share with friends back home. On holiday, they become extended outposts of their social network, scouting in order to report back in triumph.

- *Colonisers* try to set up home.

This last group is of particular interest. English colonisers are easily distinguished by the way they establish themselves abroad. The cicadas may be strumming away outside, or new fragrances floating in on the warm evening air, but the internet radio is tuned to Radio 4, providing the shipping forecast, the news and *The Archers* as audible background for drinks on the terrace. There is something reassuring about the familiarity that control of an environment brings, and for the most determined colonisers the whole domestic package, suitably scaled to fit, can be exported. Caravans and motorhomes spread out from their island base, some flying the Union Jack. Cars speed towards familiar holiday homes, hauling boxes of leaf Earl Grey to territories where the only known form of English tea comes in Liptons' bags. Such colonisers cannot comfortably stir far into the unknown without taking with them tokens of their own identity.

Some go further and put down new roots in their holiday destination. They visit the same place each year. They may decide to buy a holiday home or retirement apartment, thinking to establish a new identity in a foreign location. There is an advantage in knowing the baker on the corner, who starts baking baguettes at some ungodly hour, and it's easy to get a superficial sense of belonging, based on relationships that are, in essence, commercial. The local traders know and welcome us. But they would, wouldn't they! How deep are these roots? Is the cemetery full of our ancestors? Is theirs the language in which we habitually think? Of course not, but it's nice to fool ourselves.

Notice that there are two very different processes going on among these colonising holidaymakers. Some take tokens of home with them, forming cultural outposts wherever they go. Recreating the familiar, they export their maps of home. Standards are maintained as a sign of identity, as happened throughout the British Empire in the nineteenth century. Sometimes presented as exporting civilisation, in reality the era of empires was as much marked by attempts to maintain identity in far-flung places. There's nothing like the whiff of home when on the other side of the world. Travel around New Zealand and, sooner or later, you're bound to come across someone from Surrey or Hertfordshire!

The other process involves putting down new roots. Visitors immerse themselves in their new environment, seeking to extract identity from it. They build up a set of memories associated with this place, and thus allow it to become part of their own story, identity and evolving map.

Some are simply tempted by the ambiguous prospect of change. The Chinese philosopher Chuang Tzu dreamed that he was a butterfly, weightlessly flitting about, but woke to find himself in his usual very solid and earth-bound body. He then asked himself, 'Was I a man dreaming that I was a butterfly, or am I now a butterfly dreaming that I am a man?' There may be moments when, lulled by the sound of waves and a few drinks, towards the end of a blissful vacation, the tourist wakes on the sand and asks, 'Was I a banker dreaming of being a hippie, or am I a hippie dreaming that I used to be a banker?' New places offer the prospect of a new identity.

CHALLENGE OR SECURITY?

Nietzsche, in exploring the way in which we strive to become the Übermensch, sees such aspiration as the very opposite of that of 'the last man', who regards safety and the comfort of home as his only goal.

Might that suggest that a sense of home is antithetical to the quest for self-development? Far from it. There are two very different forms of home. One is the home within which you have tucked yourself as the price worth paying for security. We may sometimes wonder why people continue year-after-year in marriages or jobs that are so obviously limiting or damaging to their wellbeing. We assume that their need for security trumps their need to change and grow. The other form of home expresses the destination to which you are travelling, the place where you hope you will, at last, be able to be yourself. Sometimes, a change in this second form of home comes as a surprise to us and re-directs our life.

When I was in my middle teens, an elderly couple, in the village where I lived, clearly sensed that something was missing from my life. They invited me into their fifteenth century cottage, sat me down and offered me tea. I found myself in a world of which I had had no previous experience. The windows were small, the interior dark, and the ceiling timbers low, rough-cut and black. The walls were lined with bookshelves, and piles of books, papers and records threatened to invade the limited floor-space. They sat me down before a small open fire and asked if I knew any Bach. Within moments, the *St Matthew Passion* was softly filling the room. They asked what I liked to read, but I was at a loss to know how to answer. This was an utterly new world for me. But it was as if I had suddenly arrived home, I sensed that I belonged here, suddenly wanting to stay and bury myself in the books. Later, returning home, I felt strangely out of place. I certainly did not want to go and live down the road in their timber-framed cottage, but my horizon had expanded. I realised what I had been missing; my map shifted, and so did the course of my life.

Home had become dislocated – a common experience in the life-long process of growing up – and it would shift many more times in the years that lay ahead. Home was not a place of retreat, but of quest. Home was where I longed to be, even if I could not specify exactly how I wanted it to be.

When climbing a cliff, it is essential to keep at least one hand or foot on the rock face while moving the other. Climbing is incremental: you need to see and plan your next moves, while keeping securely to your existing hold. The same applies to the moves as one layer of our personal map blends into the next; we need some existing measure of security in order to find the courage to move upwards.

Homes move, change, decay, or may slowly recede from emotional view. New homes offer hope, a glimpse of a desired lifestyle, potential identity.

The sense of home is therefore time related. The security–challenge axis translates into a past–future one. Some choose to define themselves primarily by what they want rather than what they already have, by the future rather than by the past. Most are defined by both. We are thrown into this world with a set of circumstances that will largely determine our default in life, but at the same time our freedom to choose enables us – within limits – to shape our future. That was the essential message of Heidegger's *Being and Time*.

The tragedy of sudden destruction, as here in Italy following an earthquake, precipitates a crisis of loss and dislocation, but also a determination to re-build.

We need a sense of where we have come from, who we are now, and where we are going. If the past is removed, we are rootless; if the future is removed, we are hopeless; if the present is removed, we are alienated.

To know ourselves, requires a balance of past, present and future. The struggle between future hope and past nurturing is the key feature of adolescence. It is also a feature of midlife crises; if the future becomes uncertain or threatening, we may want to precipitate ourselves into something more youthful, at whatever cost. Wanting to be young again, key to such crises, is a sign that we are despairing of the future.

After many years away, I returned to live for some years in the village of my birth. The woods were familiar, the roads unchanged, the houses mostly as remembered, but often re-designed to meet changing fashions. Yet the people of my earlier years were gone – to the graveyard mostly – including the elderly couple who had introduced me to culture in their cottage. Walking among the gravestones, I am back in the world of my childhood. I know the names, even if I can no longer put faces to them. I belong to them and therefore to this place, even after many years absence. A place of ghosts can also feel like home. As a young man, I wanted to escape the village, to find space, to be comfortably anonymous. I wanted to find out who I was, and to do so unobserved. Later in life, I recognise and touch the tokens of a long-lost home.

We take all our previous homes with us, in the traces they leave on our personality, the gifts we received from them, the hurts they inflicted. We are our homes. Layer upon layer, map upon map, they make us the confused selves we become. They jostle for attention, strive for primacy and guide our shifting eyes.

At the opening of this chapter there stands a quotation from The Book of Proverbs. What does it mean to perish for lack of vision? To move forward in our map with confidence, we need some sense of the place of humankind within the universe, accepting it with all its limitations and still finding within the sphere of human activity something that is of value, noble, tragic or beautiful. By contrast, lack of vision may not literally cause us to perish, but it may certainly lead to a sense of despair, or encourage an escape into trivia.

Over time, our personal maps will change and new places of significance will be added to them, simply because we are dependent upon things over which we have no control, including the process of growing up, having family responsibilities and of ageing. The question is whether we will allow this to happen without giving it serious thought, or

149

whether we should try to be conscious of our personal space, and, by the decisions we make, nurture our sense of home.

In many ways, choosing to pay attention to our personal space is rather like making New Year's resolutions. We recognise that the new self we aspire to become is only going to be realised if we actually take steps to bring it about. It may be as simple as de-cluttering our house, adjusting our diet, or taking up some new form of exercise. By making – and keeping – resolutions we declare our intention, even in a modest way, to take the future into our own hands.

The same applies to becoming aware of the mapping out of our personal space, and locating our sense of home within it. But how do we understand the relationship we have with the world around us? That is the question to which we now turn.

Chapter 7

Engaging with our Personal Space

The world is not what I think, but what I live through.

Maurice Merleau-Ponty

How do we engage with our personal space? Let us recap our argument thus far.

We started with the mismatch between the vast and impersonal world revealed by science and cosmology and the profound human need for personal space and a sense of home, expressed through the process of what we called 'mapping'. We saw that, from a historical perspective, most societies and religions included a personal dimension in their description of the world and thereby provided scope for people to develop a sense of meaning, purpose and direction. However, with the rise of science and the dominance of a view of the world based on observation, measurement and mathematics, it became all too easy to assume that the world as analysed by science was objective and therefore 'real' whereas our personal worlds of value and meaning – whether expressed in religious or secular terms – were subjective, optional and no more than a projection of our own wishes.

This created a 'shipwreck of the heart' in which human longing for home and personal space was flung against the rocks of scientific materialism and economic and social determinism. Yet, as we saw in the last chapter, people continue to engage with the world in personal ways, and are nourished by a sense of home. To be fully human, we need to maintain a personal understanding of the world, without feeling that we are either turning our backs on reason and science, or giving way to a form of intellectual schizophrenia, which prevents the scientific and the personal from informing one another.

As a practical example of this, consider for a moment our present climate crisis. A personal interpretation of the facts suggest that, since we depend on it for life, we should think of the earth as our home, nurture it, try to minimise the damage we do to it and so on. It invites commitment and sees the climate crisis as a moral as much as a practical challenge. However, some people question the claim that human activity is a significant causal factor in global warming, and argue that we should be free to continue to exploit fossil fuels, if that improves our economic and competitive position. Factual evidence alone is unlikely to dissuade them from their view, however overwhelming it may appear to be, because they interpret it to suit their own purposes, and they accuse their opponents of doing exactly the same thing. Facts provide only the starting point for our discussion. In order to get a balanced view, we need to reflect on how we select and interpret those facts, and how they fit into our overall view of the world. In other words, the facts need to be mapped on to our world for their significance to be shown. Moral, personal and factual elements need to inform one another.

Hence, it is essential to get to grips with the way in which we engage with our personal space. It is not simply that we can thereby inject subjective elements into an otherwise objective argument, but that our personal values determine the relevant importance for us of the facts that we are to consider. Without that, those who appear vanquished in any moral debate are unlikely to concede.

If we ignore the fact that our experience is shaped by our personal space, we find ourselves negotiating our way through a complex but impersonal world. Overwhelmed by that task, we may be tempted to shrug our shoulders and ask, along with Woody Allen's boy in Brooklyn, 'What's the point?'

In this chapter, I want to argue that our fundamental problem lies with a way of thinking that divides the world up into subjective and objective, self and other, personal and impersonal. In contrast to this, I think a case can be made for seeing personal space as neither subjective nor objective, but the starting point of experience.

The concepts and values that shape our world are functional and pragmatic. They give us a means of getting through the day and making sense of life, particularly when plans fail, people die, or situations get beyond our control. Without them, a bleak and impersonal cosmos leaves us without support:

> The ancient covenant is in pieces; man at last knows that he is alone in the unfeeling immensity of the universe out of which he emerged only by chance.
>
> Jacques Monod, *Chance and Necessity*[31]

That is the bleakness against which the romantic and personal modes of thought rebel. It is not that science has been wrong in presenting the universe as unfeeling and impersonal – indeed, that is the only possible conclusion to the process of scientific analysis and measurement. But it is a universe devoid of a sense of 'home'. The complaint is not that such a universe is somehow untrue, but that it is uninhabitable.

From the Lao Tzu and the Buddha, via the Stoics and Epicureans, to Nietzsche's defiant 'yes' to life, a key feature of the quest to reduce suffering and increase happiness has been the ability to understand and accept life as it is, rather than how we would like it to be. But that is only possible if we can identify ourselves as *part of* the world within which we are embedded and engage with it in a personal way. The alternative is to see ourselves as set over against the world, which exists 'out there' as a potential source of satisfaction, an opportunity or a threat.

Scientific cosmology is brilliant at formulating explanations as to how the world has become the way it is. What it *cannot* show, however, is whether or not the world has a purpose – simply because the whole idea of 'purpose' is related to human activity. We understand the purpose of a tool, because we know the intention behind both its design and its use. But how can we understand the purpose of a galaxy or a black hole? The most we can do is relate them to more general structures and processes. To say that they have a purpose implies an intentionality that can only be applied to inanimate bodies by the most flimsy of analogies.

A virus, for example, cannot be 'cunning' or 'intelligent', even if it manages to circumvent our best endeavours to limit its spread. The most we can say is that our cunning and our intelligence is not able to predict the progress of that virus with 100% accuracy, nor put in place systems that will inhibit it. Fighting a virus is not a battle between two equally intelligent forces. Nature requires no intelligence in order to thrive, just genetic programming, growth and environmental opportunity.

So our suffering will only seem worse if we interpret what happens as unreal, or unfair, or a punishment, or as a way of isolating us, or as the result of some vindictive decision. The cancer that claims my life is not a punishment, simply a natural failure of the body's immune system to deal with cells gone rogue. We can learn from it and fight against it, but our anger at what may be happening to us can only be channelled positively if we distinguish between its personal and impersonal elements. A mutant cell or a virus does not have a personal grudge against us, even if it presents us with the ultimate challenge.

So we're caught. If we treat the universe in an entirely impersonal way, everything seems pointless; but if we treat it entirely personally, the world seems grossly unfair. How do we find a balance that allows us the satisfaction of living within our personal space? We need to start by looking at the way we experience things.

STARTING WITH EXPERIENCE

Early in the twentieth century, the philosopher Edmund Husserl (1859–1938) sought to describe what he referred to as a 'life-world', a textured, embodied world that involved emotions and memory. His approach became known as phenomenology, an attempt to understand human consciousness from a first-person point of view. Key to this was the idea that, whenever we are conscious of something, we take in not just the sensations we have of it – colour, taste, sound and so on – but also the meaning it has for us; its significance. We are conscious, not just of objects out there in the world, but of our way of relating to them, and of our own actions with regard to them.

He also introduced the idea of intentionality. When we give attention to something, we understand it in terms of our existing thoughts, ideas and images. We do not just experience something, but experience it 'as' something – we give it significance and, in our very act of experiencing it, set up our relationship with it. To give a practical example: I cannot observe a lemon being sliced, the clonk as a couple of ice cubes hit the bottom of a glass, the glug of gin being poured and the fizzing sound of tonic being sloshed over it, without thinking of the delight of drinking a gin and tonic! My stance towards that set of experiences is most definitely intentional – I am not going to remain a detached observer of each element in that particular sequence!

Phenomenology suggests that we take an intentional stance towards everything. That is what creates our life-world, or *Lebenswelt* in German. We do not first observe and understand something and only then decide how we will relate to it. Our relationship to the new object, fact or information comes along with our experience of it. So, human experience is always going to be very different from scientific measurement. Apart from anything else, it comes theory-laden; we understand it in terms of our existing views. We also bring to it our unique perspective: our hopes, fears, intentions, values, likes and dislikes.

ENFRAMING AND AUTHENTICITY

Martin Heidegger (1889–1976) was one of the most remarkable and controversial philosophers of the twentieth century, and one who – as we have already seen in his comments about building and dwelling – has a great deal to contribute to our understanding of home and personal space, even if the style of his written philosophy can be, to put it politely, challenging!

His seminal work, *Being and Time* (1927), is a key text for understanding both personal space and the political dangers that lurk within a very traditional sense of home, which we shall consider in the next chapter. For Heidegger, we are thrown at birth into a particular time and place; we have a finite existence and live aware of the fact that, one day, we are going to die. But our experience is of being alive in this world here and now – that is our starting point.

He therefore refers to a human being as *Dasein*, a German term meaning something like 'being-there'. It refers to the self that is experienced prior to the division between subject and object. I am a being in the world, not a separate thinking self, nor a physical being that can be exhaustively described in terms of physics and biology. *Dasein* is what it means to be me, present and embedded in my world.

As we look around the world, we give things value and meaning as they relate to us. A tree is not just a tree, but perhaps also a source of fruit, or shade, or building material, or firewood. In other words, when we experience something, we put it in a frame. This process, which Heidegger called 'enframing', operates at every level. So, for example, he suggests that science enframes the world in terms of calculability; it reduces everything to numbers and relationships, its analysis demystifies everything, reducing it to a calculation. On the person-to-person level, we enframe others and are ourselves enframed – as a mother, a child, a relative, a friend, a customer, a client, a consumer, a citizen, a representative, a member, a stranger, an interloper, a spy, an object of hate or adulation, a non-entity on the roadside.

We understand things in terms of what they can do for us or mean for us. We never see things objectively, but always in ways that personalise our experience of them and show their relevance.

In considering this kind of perspective, one of the key works in twentieth century philosophy, although brief, is Thomas Nagel's *The View from Nowhere*, published in 1986. The question he addressed was how we reconcile our own particular viewpoints with the kind of objective view, the 'view from nowhere' that science claims to present. As I engage with life, I do so from my particular perspective, and that is going to be different from everyone else's. What is more, from my perspective, I am the centre of the world – things at a distance are less important to me than those close at hand. But I know that, objectively speaking, my own existence and perspective is insignificant. Any attempt at objectivity, particularly in science and cosmology, puts me in my place, and a very small place it is.

But science is value-free and perspective-free only if we choose to make it so. In practice, the way we engage with science, and the questions we ask of it, determine what it yields. This was illustrated time and again during the 2020 pandemic, where politicians claimed to be 'following the science' when what they were actually doing was choosing how to interpret and make use of scientific facts. Choices depend on facts only once they are mediated by values. We decide what is acceptable from the various options that science presents.

The problem comes when we try to 'enframe' the world as a whole. It is too vast. We cannot find any definitive values within it. Many have tried to use evolution as the ultimate key to value, but not only is that a ruthless process far removed from personal intuitions of right and wrong, but evolution on this planet is itself rendered ultimately insignificant in the light of the processes at work within the wider cosmos. The attempted 'view from nowhere' remains chilling.

Hence, the personal and the impersonal are two very different ways of engaging with the world. This basic fact about human experience was eloquently described by the Jewish philosopher Martin Buber. In *I and Thou* (1923) he distinguished between the 'I-it' of impersonal experience and the 'I-thou' of the personal. So, even if science and objectivity are incredibly useful in the way we understand and manipulate the world around us, they do not and cannot have the last word. For the most important aspects of life demand a particular and personal viewpoint. To see everything in terms of 'it' is to face alienation.

If we 'enframe' things, people and experiences in terms of what they mean for us, it is logical that we also enframe places. The places that are most important for us – places we associate with friends or family, with happy times or traumatic, with memories that remain painful or comfortably enriching – make us who we are and shape our personal map.

A world in which nothing was enframed, would be like a featureless desert. But while enframing gives significance to individual things in our world, our mapping shows their relationship to one another and to us.

Heidegger was particularly concerned that we should act with authenticity – in other words, that we should 'be ourselves' and not simply follow convention. For him, to do as 'one does' is to live in an inauthentic way and to live behind a social mask. This determination, to free ourselves from the restraints of convention, became the central theme of existentialism, when it took Paris by storm in the late 1940s and made Sartre something of a celebrity. Heidegger, never willing to be labelled existentialist and dismissing the likes of Sartre, nevertheless provided, in the concepts of enframing and authenticity, the fundamental structure both for existentialism and for our understanding of personal space, home and identity. Our choices make us who we are; we should not accept the way others choose to enframe us. I am more than a customer, or a parent, and I will never live authentically if I simply try to imitate what I think a good customer or parent should be. I have to be myself and accept the consequences.

Clearly, this has implications for our idea of 'home'. It is not something that we are simply given when we are thrown into life, but something we need to commit to and 'own'. If my home is not authentic, neither am I. There is nothing sadder than those who claim that their situation is totally the result of circumstances; that they had no choice; that they simply did what was expected of them. It may be true, but that does not stop it being sad.

There is a wonderful Buddhist comment, attributed to the 8th century scholar Shantideva, and utterly relevant in a world where roads are rough. He asks, 'Where will I find enough leather to cover the whole world?' but then comments, 'With just the leather of my sandals, it is as if the whole world were covered'. The attempt to change the world to suit our needs will always be beyond our ability, but if we can change ourselves, our world will appear different.

That sounds remarkably similar to the Stoic view:
    Some things are within our power, while others are not.
    Within our power are opinion, motivation, desire,

aversion, and, in a word, whatever is of our own doing; not within our power are our body, our property, reputation, office, and, in a word, whatever is not of our own doing.

Epictetus Enchiridion 1.1

Epictetus himself put his philosophy into practice, triumphing over his personal circumstances. He started life as a slave and was crippled, but in spite of that he developed a passion for philosophy, improved his situation and eventually obtained his freedom. He then set himself up as a teacher of philosophy in Rome until, in 93 ACE, the Emperor Domitian banned all philosophers. Not to be thwarted by such an edict, Epictetus moved to Greece and set up a school of philosophy there, living modestly into old age and continuing his passion for teaching philosophy. I presume Shantideva did not know of him, but, if he had, he would certainly have admired his ability to make sandals!

The same principle applies to our map of life. It is of little use complaining that our 'home' is inadequate, and that, if only things had been different, we would have succeeded in so many ways. Our external circumstances are not of our choosing, but how we understand our 'home' within them depends on our personal choices. Home is therefore an existential question, not a physical or historical one.

Following a rather Biblical image, Heidegger speaks of the 'fallenness' of a being 'lost' in the world, and of the angst of not being 'at home' in the world.[32] Here, Heidegger's language brings together the implications of our 'thrown' nature, and the danger of becoming inauthentic by behaving in a way that simply conforms to other people's expectations. He describes the plight of such a person as being 'lost'. The implication being that we can only be 'at home', in ourselves and our world, if we take personal responsibility for the choices we make.

So, if an exclusively scientific paradigm starves the world of the personal dimension, and if we recognise the way in which we enframe things and strive for authenticity, how should we understand and interpret our experience? What does it mean for something to be both true in itself and true 'for me?' Without an honest attempt to answer that question, we are in deep trouble.

PRIMITIVE CONTACT

The French existentialist philosopher Maurice Merleau-Ponty (1908–61), developing the phenomenology of Husserl, sought to achieve 'a direct and primitive contact with the world' and to give accounts of the world 'as we live them'.

He accepted that science was constructed from our experience of the world, but wanted to get beyond it, complaining that 'I cannot shut myself up within the realm of science.' And here is his key to our new way of looking at the world:[33]

> To return to things in themselves is to return to that world which precedes knowledge, of which knowledge always *speaks*, and in relation to which every scientific schematisation is an abstract and derivative sign language, as is geography in relation to the countryside in which we have learned beforehand what a forest, a prairie or a river is.[34]

We need to pause and reflect on the implication of this. Most of the time we accept that science is able to show us the world in an objective way; that it gives us reality itself, rather than some subjective or personal view of our own. But Merleau-Ponty is arguing that such a view is wrong, because it seems to present a gulf between what we perceive and reality, so that the latter becomes unknowable, as had been argued by Immanuel Kant. His view is summed up in two quotes from the preface to his *Phenomenology of Perception*:

We must not, therefore, wonder whether we really perceive a world, we must indeed say: the world is what we perceive.

The world is not what I think, but what I live through.

In other words, we *live* in the world before we start philosophising or analysing it. The world is the place within which we are embedded; the environment within which we are nourished. We cannot stand aside from it, because we are already in the midst of it.

I cannot therefore define the place that will be my home. Rather, 'home' is the word that describes the cluster of experiences within which I sense I belong. We discover it; we do not plan for it.

To separate the self from its environment, peering out at the world from our inner sanctum, is to adopt a bunker mentality. As here at Verdun, a bunker may be a shelter, but it can never be a home. To be nourished and at home, we need to live in constant interaction with the world around us.

'Home' is something we already know – either as a reality, or a longing, or a sense of deep regret or of nostalgia. To paraphrase Merleau-Ponty's way of putting it, we should not ask, 'do I belong at home?' but simply recognise that 'home is where I belong'.

Perhaps the most elegant way of describing the distinction between the personal and impersonal aspects of space comes from another French writer, Gaston Bachelard, as set out in his *Poetics of Space* (French edition, 1958). He applied phenomenology to architecture, exploring the emotional engagement we have with buildings and parts of buildings. He explores images, and the impact of the imagination on the way we understand the spaces within which we live. His ideas have been influential within art, architecture and philosophy, and he is not afraid to draw into his idea of constructed space, ideas gleaned from literature, and a broad appreciation of culture and community.

You cannot imagine two styles of writing more different than Bachelard's and Heideggers's, and yet they point in the same direction – that we can only understand space and time, and the world within which we live, if we do so in a way that is personal and imaginative. To dwell somewhere is a far richer experience than simply being located in that place, it is to bring to it a sense of home.

SPACES AND PLACES

In 1977, a Professor of Geography, Yi-Fu Tuan published a book entitled *Space and Place*,[35] exploring human geography. In it he made a crucial distinction between *space*, as that through which we move, and *place*, which refers to a known location. A process of understanding the world is therefore one in which we create and know places within space. He argues that, on the one hand, we are attracted to a sense of place, as somewhere that offers security or a place to know and be known whereas, on the other hand, space offers a sense of freedom and movement.

That distinction has implications for our understanding of home. In so far as it is a place, home offers security and self-definition; home is who you are and where you belong. But we are restless, we want to explore, to make more of ourselves, push the boundaries of our life. And that restlessness is expressed in the need for space. The teenager finds home claustrophobic, the entrepreneur seeks to grow beyond the old family business. The youngster wants to pack up and travel the world, to get a sense of space and experience what it is like to be in new places. That exploration of space – of freedom to move from one place to another – is a natural part of growing up.

So we need a place, whether physical, social or mental, that we think of as home, but without being cramped by it, and with the possibility of exploring beyond it. With apologies to Kipling, one might say, 'what do they know of home, who only home know?'

A sense of security may be important here. All that is unexpected or threatening is tamed by being seen as part of a cosmology, having a place in a known and understood world, so that:

> 'Space is transformed into place as it acquires definition and meaning.'[36]

Notice how someone who is ill tends to want to be 'home' and surrounded by all that is familiar. Distances are covered in a journey, but it is the places that are encountered that give it meaning. We remember places, but we also remember passing through the spaces between them, relating them to one another.

The word 'home' carries with it a primary sense of security and acceptance. At its best it can be what the Dutch describe as *gezellig*. A literal translation might be 'cosy', but it means more than that. It's sitting down together with a coffee, gathering with family and friends in an atmosphere that oozes comfortable, friendly inclusiveness. Consider the sort of place or room that, for you, would suggest a location for many a *gezellige* time with family or friends. Clean, minimalist, expansive and outward-looking? Small, womb-like, furnished in rich, Victorian, colours? Which would be more important for you: the view out from your room, or the sense that your

164

room shelters you from the cold world outside? Imagining that room, which takes priority – sunlight streaming in, or logs burning on the fire?

One of the challenges in creating a personal space is to find a way of allowing it to express our own personality, while at the same time – if that is what we want – making it a place of welcome for others.

In contrasting the local with the universal, in our sense of place, Tuan comments on the implication this has for religion:

> Religion could either bind a people to a place or free them from it. The worship of local gods binds a people to place, whereas universal religions give freedom.[37]

Here I'd part company from Tuan. He implies that, for a universal religion, no one place is any more sacred than any other. If that were so, it would be difficult to name a universal religion: Christianity has its places of pilgrimage and its sacred architecture; Islam has a very special relationship with Mecca, with orientation to that place a central feature of prayer; Judaism has it, perhaps supremely the Western Wall in Jerusalem, but also the scrolls of the Torah within each synagogue. Monotheism, however universal in its reach, thrives on particular places and special objects.

Tuan tends to see the world in static terms, arguing that we could not develop a sense of place if we see everything as a process. But some, including the French scientist and theologian Teilhard de Chardin, have done just that – locating the point of significance, not at a physical location in the present, but at the final point of an evolutionary movement. If your aspirations are the focus of your life, your home is always going to be located in the future.

The distinction between space and place has not always been made in this way. An alternative approach was taken in the 1980s by Michel de Certeau.[38] He described space as that which is experienced and colonised, while place is the physical location in which space develops. But here, although the words are interchanged, the distinction remains the same.

An alternative set of terms is provided by Maurice Merleau-Ponty, who distinguishes between undifferentiated 'geometrical space' and 'anthropological space'. It strikes me that 'anthropological space' is simply a more scientific or detached way of saying 'personal space'. So his terminology is closer to the one we adopt in this book, and that of Tuan, than to that of Michel de Certeau. As we have already seen, for Merleau-Ponty all perception is theory-laden. We categorise and understand what we encounter, on the basis of our existing view of the world and we always understand things in terms of what they mean *for us*. And this, of course, links back to Heidegger's idea of 'enframing'.

Would you buy a house if it offered no more than 'undifferentiated geometrical space'? I think not. Our intention, as we look at any space and imagine ourselves within it, is that it should be 'enframed' as our home

GIVING DIRECTIONS

In his exploration of personal space, Michel de Certeau distinguishes between a 'map' or a 'tour'. Whereas a map attempts to set out various personal spaces in a way that shows their relationship to one another – this is to the right of that, and so on – a tour consists of a set of directions. It suggests that you turn right here or go straight on there; it guides you through the terrain.

That distinction rather assumes that a map waits to be unfolded in front of you, so that you can then cast your eyes around it in order to get your bearings. But our description of mapping is not like that; it is a process by which we set out the things that are important for us. The map is not presented as ready made, but is constantly being re-drawn. As soon as I add something new to my map, everything else shifts to accommodate it. How does that work?

166

Imagine you are enthused by *Strictly Come Dancing* and decide that, more than anything else, you want to learn to dance. You arrange to take lessons; you spend time practising at home; you watch programmes about dance. You may eventually pluck up courage and start going to public dances in order to practice your new skills. That's all fine; you have chosen to add 'dancing' to your personal map. But it is likely that, as you become involved with your new interest, other things will recede a little in their importance for you. Your stamp collection is no longer your all-absorbing interest!

In that way, we are the ones giving the directions. Although influenced by our existing maps, those direction shape our maps as we go forward. If we get into a new relationship, or get married, or start a family, or change career, or retire, our maps will shift radically. Looking back, we may be quite surprised to find that some things that had previously been important in our lives, have receded or vanished completely.

So the map shifts with every decision we make, just as the satnav in my car recalculates every time I diverge from its suggested route. Our mapping and re-mapping is constantly fed by new experiences and choices. No satnav would be of use if it did no more than analyse the route already taken. It needs to be given a destination and the information necessary for it to assess possible routes. A satnav suggests what to do next, in the light of what you have previously done.

The landscape around us may shift, with economic circumstances or the coming of a virus – things that are outside our control – but it is by choosing what is important for us, within each new situation, that we influence the mapping of our personal space and sense of home.

In effect, by attaching value and meaning to a space, we turn it into a place. That space can be a physical one (a room, a house, a city, a nation even), or a social or mental one (a career, a political party, a local community, a passion for some activity or organisation through which our interest can be channelled). It may be a particular shop, or café or bar, a corner of the street, or a place where we have been on holiday – all can be transformed from something neutral and impersonal, into somewhere we value and which therefore becomes part of our world.

SYMBOLS OF THE PERSONAL

Objects become symbolic when they point beyond themselves, reminding us of particular people, values, ideas, places or events. Hence, when we look round a room that we have made our own, we have the sense of who we are and where we have come from, because we can take a mental check on the symbols within our field of vision.

Devoid of personal symbols, a hotel room may be luxurious, but it cannot be a home. Yet in each of the identical flats in a vast, impersonal block, people may create a sense of home by filling it with things that have special meaning for them. Whether it is in a shed, a loved patch of garden, or the corner of a room, people can surround themselves with symbols that reinforce their sense of self.

I used to work in a hospital, and found that people's lives were often set out on the lockers by their bedside. Photos of family and friends, gifts, cards, books, fruit; each item, small in itself, served as a symbol for a whole slice of life outside the world of the hospital. Some lockers and tables were utterly cluttered; some almost bare. You can learn a lot from a locker.

But this personalising process may go into reverse. We destroy the personal nature of space whenever we regard it as a commodity. We may be tempted to buy a particular house or flat, not because it has personal significance for us, or has been the focus of our family, but because it promises to offer a certain status and style of living, or to prove a good medium-term investment. We buy personal space on an impersonal prospectus; only after we have bought it do we engage with the optional task of turning a house into a home. Equally, a home may be dismantled, if treated impersonally.

One of the saddest things about clearing out the possessions of someone who has died, is disposing of their personal stuff. The long-treasured vase is deemed worthless, and goes to a charity shop, just in case someone can be found to give it a home. On the other hand, a grandparent's retirement watch, used every day and a constant reminder of a lifetime in the same company, may be worth sending to auction, where it will go to the highest bidder, probably a dealer. Its price will be established, its previous value completely forgotten.

The symbols of our personal space come and go. Some items are cherished and take on a value and meaning far in excess of their monetary worth, while others are no longer wanted and can therefore be reduced to their cash value.

CREATIVITY

Creativity may blossom as a result of achieving a sense of home, or finding inspiration within one's personal space. Friedrich Nietzsche, for example, came to see the village of Sils-Maria, high in the Alps, as his intellectual and spiritual home. He needed height. He needed the thin atmosphere, clean air and the sense that he was in a dangerous zone where eagles swoop and get their superior view of the ground below. While there, he walked – as have many philosophers – in order to think. Thinking can therefore require both a place and movement. Even pacing up and down can free up blocked thought. We need to be free, to move, to climb, to attain some sort of view over the landscape. We may need space in order to allow our creativity to flourish.

Would you settle for a hut in the mountains as your source of inspiration?

Simplicity and remoteness can also release creativity. Henry David Thoreau's musings on the simple life, gathered in his *Walden; or, Life in the Woods* describe the time he spent living a life of self-sufficiency beside Walden Pond, in Concord, Massachusetts, from 1845–7. His cultivation of solitude was a deliberate attempt to see if he could lead a satisfying and fulfilling life separated from other people. He created his own personal space, clearly happy to feel himself at one with the natural world around him.

The philosophy that underpinned his experiment, which he shared with his friend Ralph Waldo Emerson, is termed 'Transcendentalism'. It used people's intuition about what was right for them, to explore how society might change in order to promote the development of each individual, reckoning that people were actually aware of themselves and their world in a way that transcended their ordinary day-to-day experience, and that they were at their best when independent and self-reliant. It assumed a fundamental goodness, both in people and in nature – a goodness that was restricted by conforming to the norms of social life, but released by independent living. It had practical as well as intellectual implications that, for Thoreau, involved building his own log cabin by the lake and living the simple life. It was, as much as anything, an exploration of the way in which personal space can be cultivated.

His most-quoted comment, from early in the book, is that 'the mass of men live lives of quiet desperation' – contrasting the constant pursuit of status and money, with his quest for simplicity. He contrasts the cabin he constructed with most dwellings:

> Most men appear never to have considered what a house is, and are actually though needlessly poor all their lives because they think that they must have such a one as their neighbors have.

Although published in the 1850s, I doubt he would have changed his views if he could have seen the rows of new executive homes springing up to meet the aspirations of the newly wealthy of the twenty-first century, nor consider the way in which property is regarded as a form of investment. We could well argue that, in the quest for an ever-better house, many people suffer lives of quiet mortgage desperation. Thoreau points to the simple fact that housing can become a means of self-identity, but, surely, to want a place 'such as their neighbors have' is also a way of gaining identity. In societies where class distinctions still matter, it is possible to buy a property that suggests we belong to one class, while displaying the telltale signs that suggest we actually come from another. There are some social circles, into which one cannot 'buy' a place, although in a society dominated by the power of money, their numbers are shrinking fast. What appears to be the quest for a nicer home, may actually be little more than the purchase of a stepping stone by an upwardly-mobile itinerant.

Thoreau contrasts his house with one that is constructed for the purely utilitarian purpose of offering shelter, and yet such

171

a view would seem rather indulgent; after all, it is one thing to deliberately choose simplicity of housing for a limited period of time, quite another to have such simplicity imposed by poverty. But one feature of his housing reflects all that this book went on to argue: that he deliberately chose where he would live and for what purpose. His was not an accidental house, or one pressed upon him by the demands of his social position. This was exactly what he wanted, and it therefore reflected who he was. He chose a 'space' and made of it a 'place', and that sense of ownership allowed him the leisure to expand on his philosophy of simplicity and pragmatism.

But Thoreau was certainly not the first to seek a place away from the clutter of life. In the early centuries of Christianity, monastic seclusion in the desert was seen as an ideal place for spiritual insight. And this persists in the benefits offered by de-cluttering one's personal space, or by clarifying the mind through meditation or going on a retreat, whether religious or secular.

Some lucky creators can work whatever their circumstances, but others require the personal workspace to be just right. For writers, it may be the type of pen, or colour of paper, or choice of word-processor or font. For some it's a matter of the right time of day or night, or the need for seclusion, even if just a room of one's own. The concepts of personal space and of home therefore apply to particular activities as well as life in general. Get the personal space right, and the juices can flow.

THE JOINED-UP WORLD

Creativity, whether of the artistic kind or simply getting on with everyday activities, engages with the world in a way that is quite different from scientific observation. Nature is an interconnected, ever-changing web of events; but, seen through the eyes of science and reason, we divide it up into discrete objects and explore the relationship between them. We speak of one thing or event being 'caused' by another, and thereby consider it explained. But in reality, all such causality needs to be qualified, for every cause has its own causes, and those spread outwards from any single event until they embrace the whole universe. Discrete entities and exclusive causes are features of the way our minds work, not of how the world is. Causes appear when we extract a limited number of events, and calculate which follow from which on a regular basis. Causality, as David Hume pointed out, is a habit of mind, but it has become deeply embedded in our consciousness and thus a necessary feature of all experience, as Immanuel Kant argued.

Stand back from that analysis, however, and our experience becomes more complicated. I may start by thinking of myself as a separate object, relating to a world that is outside me and about which I am informed by my senses. But I cannot deny that I am also *part of* that world – I act; I change or avoid things; I eat, breed, survive and grow; eventually, if I survive that long, I will become old and die. But my experience of being is not the same as an objective, analytic description of what it is to be. In that way of thinking, I become no more than the firing of neurones and the processing of food and oxygen, a complex machine, set within a larger machine. The 'I' of my engaged experience is nowhere to be found.

We only reinstate the 'I' of self-awareness once we choose to interpret the world in personal terms and give it value. Self and world form a necessary pair. Once they separate – once I stop feeling part of the world but only an observer of the world – I am lost in space, confronted by an impersonal and meaningless universe; I no longer have a place where I belong.

But that's not how life is, or needs to be. Once we acknowledge and take responsibility for our personal space, we engage with life more directly and creatively. But, of course, life has a social dimension that cannot be ignored. Our sense of home has profound political consequences, both good and bad, to which we need to turn.

Are there people in there? Yes. Are their lives influenced by the design of the building within which they work? Perhaps. Is it an exciting place to be? Again, perhaps. The one thing we do know, however, is that, for human flourishing, each of them will need some sense of home, some set of values to give orientation within his or her world.

Chapter 8

The Politics of Personal Space

Homelessness is coming to be the destiny of the world.
Martin Heidegger[39]

I was mesmerised by the terrain over which we were passing. The plane was equipped with a camera under the fuselage and its view of the ground, thousands of feet below, was a slow-moving option on the little screen in front of me.

Although many years have elapsed, I shall never forget that flight, returning to the UK from Japan. We headed up through northern China and across Mongolia into Siberia. For hour after hour, there was nothing below us but wilderness – mile upon mile of mountain ranges, snow, ice sheets, and then the frozen lakes and drab vastness of the Russian tundra. It was astoundingly beautiful but hostile; a cruelly inhospitable Garden of Eden before the arrival of Adam.

Then, as we tracked westwards towards Moscow, I saw the first human traces – pipelines heading back from the Siberian waste, then the first roads, straight lines scored across the wilderness to the horizon. Far from being comforting, they only served to emphasise the remoteness of the land across which they stretched. Then the odd building appeared, outposts of the human world, then towns of increasing size, and finally the grey smear of the outskirts of Moscow itself appeared beneath us in the haze. Before long we were over the Baltic and then in slow descent across the Netherlands. The terrain over which we were now passing had been totally re-shaped by humankind: neatly ploughed fields, woods, factories, motorways and huge swathes of suburbia, spread thickly over the land. Below us were straight lines, organised junctions, the gathered pattern of cities with their unfurling sprawls of housing, water flowing in ordered channels over reclaimed land – all utterly unlike the pristine ice and low scrub of a few hours earlier.

For me, that flight recreated, over the span of a few hours, a visual representation of the warming and colonising process of human development over the last 12,000 years, from the barren northern landscape of the last ice age, through the gradual spreading of humankind, to a modern world of commodified and personalised space. Like it or not, we are part of a fine-meshed but fragile human net thrown over the planet, within which our existence is essentially communal and our lives interconnected.

On reflection, however, that interconnected web was only half the story. The other half concerns what happens when our sense of political identity loses touch with our personal space.

For many people, the idea of being defined by their home has become problematic. We may move regularly, have friends all over, commute a distance to our workplace, where we meet with other circles of friends or at least acquaintances. Some are accused of being more 'at home' in the office than in their own home. Some use work or hobbies to escape a home that does not provide them with the identity they need. Some just have a low boredom threshold when it comes to places to live. Some see themselves as genuinely cosmopolitan; if a better job is offered in Hong Kong or Sydney, they'll go – and, after all, they expect to meet up with circles of like-minded people when they get there, and they can always return regularly to visit friends and relatives. It's a small world – you can live anywhere and stay in touch!

One attraction of such cosmopolitanism is the refusal to be limited by a label. The ancient Greek thinker, Diogenes of Sinope (404–323BCE), the first Cynic philosopher, best known for living in a barrel with provocative disregard for social convention, refused to say to which city, or *polis*, he belonged and therefore declared himself to be a citizen of the world, a 'cosmopolitan'.

But is that attitude emotionally and intellectually sustainable? We may defy the conventions of one place, but in doing so – emotionally, if not physically – we tend to identify ourselves with another. I may reject the narrowness of a childhood home, only to adopt the hedonistic rules of student life. Diogenes claims to be cosmopolitan because he thinks globally; his map is larger than that of most people of his day, so he can afford to become a rebel and a non-conformist.

Our thinking about the social and political world cannot be disinterested or objective; that way lies the madness of thinking we can control the uncontrollable, playing chess with independently motivated pieces. The truth we seek needs to be engaged, rather than analytic – truth for me, truth upon which I can act, truth that speaks not just to my mind, but to my emotions. But can I become cosmopolitan without also having some sense of home from which to start my journey of exploration? I love the variety of cultures, languages and styles of food and dress – uniformity (as we see too often in globalised retail offerings) would be boring – but my enjoyment of all these things, and of the sense of adventure when travelling, is based on a prior sense of who I am, on my 'home'. To travel with no prior identity is to drift rather than to explore.

However, I disagree with the quotation from Heidegger that stands at the head of this chapter. Seeing the world as increasingly mechanised and globalised, he feared that this would inevitably lead to a kind of homelessness. As we shall see, that is indeed the threat of the globalising and impersonal tendency in the world today, but I sense that its threat will always be countered by a resurgence of commitment to what is particular and local, with results that may be either beneficial or seriously damaging. Heidegger saw what was coming, but not our reaction to it, which has already set its dangerous stamp upon the twenty-first century.

However, in order to appreciate the personal implications of this, we need to step back and consider a fundamental moral issue that threatens to destabilise our political sense of home, an issue that originated almost two and a half thousand years ago in China.

THE CHALLENGE OF MO TZU

Mo Tzu, a Confucian philosopher born in the fifth century BCE, challenged the established view of the society of his day. Confucius had placed great emphasis on respect and family loyalty. Although he proposed a version of the 'Golden Rule', namely that you should avoid doing to others what you would not wish them to do to you, he believed that one should give priority to one's own family and also show respect to those in authority. For Confucius, society formed a natural hierarchy, so that, although he saw the need for courtesy and correct behaviour towards everyone, it was first of all necessary for people to know their place and to act accordingly. The implication of his social hierarchy and culture of respect, was that it was both unreasonable and unnatural to attempt to treat everyone in the same way.

Mo Tzu, however, claimed that particular concern for one's own family, at the expense of equal goodwill towards all, was at the root of all social evils. Whereas Confucius' version of the Golden Rule was essentially negative, avoiding harm, Mo Tzu wanted to make it positive, treating everyone equally. Forgetting any prior commitment to kinship or rank, every action should be judged on the basis of whether or not it

178

helped society as a whole. He agued that people should live more frugally, rather than waste their resources on lavish ceremonies, particularly on funeral rites.

In effect, Mo Tzu was a utilitarian, more than two thousand years before Jeremy Bentham set down his principle of utility. He sought a society based on the greatest good for the greatest number, rather than one based on hierarchy and family loyalty.

But is it realistic to expect us to seek the greatest happiness for the greatest number? Is it not more natural for us to care most for people who are like ourselves, particularly our close friends and family?

To take the most obvious example; suppose you see a group of children struggling in deep water and in immediate danger of drowning. You have a chance to save only one of them. Would it really be a matter of indifference to you which of them you tried to save, if one of them was your own child? Could you, in that moment of crisis, really opt to pluck another child from the water and leave your own to drown? Could you look back, seeing your own child pleading for help, and not feel utterly torn? Would you not, in that fearful moment, see flashing before your mind's eye all those precious times that you shared with that child since his or her birth? Does your own child not occupy a unique place on your personal map, unlike the other children in distress? From a utilitarian perspective, it would require great moral courage to opt to save the child of a stranger, but could you live with yourself if you did so?

Rationally, you might applaud the idea of treating all alike, reducing your own goods to the level of the poorest, and behaving towards complete strangers as you would your own family and friends, but could you actually do it? That is the challenge human nature poses both to Mo Tzu and to modern utilitarianism. Whatever reason may say, our natural instinct is to prioritise care for our own family and friends.

Observe other species and we see the willingness of parents to sacrifice themselves for the sake of their offspring, with whom they have a unique relationship. Penguins, returning to their colony after feeding out at sea, can detect the particular cry of their own chick among thousands of – to human eyes – apparently identical ones. Does that indicate that they are insufficiently evolved, and that eventually they will maximise the number who can survive, by sharing their regurgitated fish equally among all the chicks in the colony? However agonisingly painful it is to watch some young animals die while others are flourishing, we have to accept that such kinship priority is deeply embedded in the survival mechanism of many species, humans included.

Common sense suggests that, without particular commitments and variations in the value we give to things, we have no basis for choice or action. How do we decide anything, if all options are equally important and appealing? It is precisely because I value some things and people more than others, that I can choose what to do. We therefore need to strike a balance between the universal and the particular, between being a citizen of the world and one of a particular culture, nation and city.

But, if a genuinely personal cosmopolitan vision is problematic, so also is the alternative. To limit our sense of 'home' to one particular place, makes us equally vulnerable, because everything – whether a locality, a religion or a political creed – will eventually change beyond recognition and finally disappear. That is a fact of life, and any philosophy that pretends it is not the case is delusional and probably pathological. Hitler's Third Reich, destined at its launch to last a thousand years, managed to survive just twelve. Most projects touted as 'world beating' end up as failures. Tomorrow's promised bestseller will one day be remaindered. I knew, as soon as my publisher started to describe me as a 'bestselling author' on the back cover of my books, that I was doomed to decline. Linking our supposed eternal destiny to a particular person, place or idea is a recipe for disappointment, if not disaster.

STOIC MAPPING

One answer to Mo Tzu's challenge can be found in the writings of the Stoics of ancient Greece. They considered the whole world to be rationally ordered, and therefore recommended that human beings should consider their place within it and act accordingly. Hence, they believed that everyone belonged to the family of humankind and should be treated with equal justice, giving rational underpinning to the Cynic Diogenes' view that he was 'cosmopolitan' rather than committed only to one particular *polis*. Zeno of Citium (c 334–262 BCE), founder of the Stoic school of philosophy, used the term *oikeiôsis* to describe something that belongs to you, or to which you are committed. The word derives from *oikos*, meaning a house or a domestic setting, and therefore refers to the sense of 'home' in the things with which we identify. But how can we move beyond such personal commitments to treat all equally? The clue lies in a development of this idea of *oikeiôsis*.

In the second century, the Stoic philosopher Hierocles took up the idea of *oikeiôsis*, arguing that 'each of us is ... circumscribed by many circles'.[40] The closest of these concentric circles is that of one's own mind and body, but surrounding it comes the circle of brothers and sisters, parents and other close relatives, and then, in a third, he places grandparents and cousins. Beyond these comes the circle of the people who belong to your own city, then your own province, until, finally, there is the circle representing the whole human race.

So far; so Confucius. But, for Hierocles, the ethical implication of this is that we should train ourselves to care about those in the outer circles as though they were in the inner ones. We should try to be as morally committed to the welfare of someone on the other side of the world, as we would be to a near neighbour.

In this way, he gives practical expression to the 'mapping' process we outlined earlier. He recognises the way in which we construct the concentric circles of awareness, and then applies ethical logic to say how this should lead us to treat others, allowing our natural commitments to spread outwards, from our own family and friends, through our neighbourhood and nation, towards the global community.

This Stoic approach gives a practical way of overcoming our present dilemma. The leap from emotional particularity to utilitarian globalism is just too great, and appears to pit the immediate and local against the universal. If it's either/or, we know that, for all but the utilitarian hero, the immediate and local tends to win. But if we gradually work our way outwards through the circles of things with which we identify, we take the personal element with us as we approach global issues.

In other words, following Stoic advice, we should train ourselves to think globally without negating our commitment to those near to us. It should not be an either/or calculation, but a both/and enlargement of the circles with which we identify.

There is an ethical parallel to this in the Buddhist tradition. In a meditation that aims to develop compassion, Buddhists are encouraged to think of every creature as if it were their own mother. That may prove a bit of a stretch of the meditative imagination, and it rather depends on our relationship with our own mother, but the end result is exactly that encouraged by Hierocles. Both traditions seek to enlarge the awareness of our commitments to others based on our own sense of belonging, whether that is through perception, logical reflection or meditation.

So our idea of home can expand outwards, through concentric circles of personal space, each populated by those people, things and ideas that give shape to who we are. It
182

provides a starting point for politics and ethics, without falling into the utilitarian trap of assuming we can simply legislate for equality and hope that human nature will fall into line. The Stoic/Buddhist approach here may avoid the social and political equivalent of 'the breath of empty space', namely the atomisation of society.

SOCIAL ATOMISM

In chapter five, we looked at the way Copernicus, Galileo, Bacon, Newton and others transformed the older view of the world, introducing modern science based on reason and observation. That shift started a process that led to the clash between our personal need to be 'at home' in our world, and the threat of an impersonal universe.

But the seventeenth century saw an equally radical shift in the view of society and the individual, highlighted in a shift in ideas between those of Thomas Hobbes (1588–1679) and John Locke (1637–1704), a shift towards the introduction of what was to become representative democracy.

Before the spread of modern democracy, most societies – even when they operated under direct democratic control, as in ancient Athens – were organised as a hierarchy. Typically, at the summit was the king, emperor, tribal chief or whatever, whose authority was given by God, and below him (or, rarely, her) came nobles, landowners and so on down to the common people. In such a world, your life opportunities were largely inherited and determined by your rank. You had relatively little prospect of changing your social status, although of course there were always exceptions. Whether maintained by divine will or raw secular power, it was broadly speaking a society based on tradition and imposed values. Your personal space in that society was given rather than chosen.

At the very bottom of that hierarchy, in many societies, came the slaves. Deprived of rights, owned and used as human tools, they were effectively dehumanised. The act of returning freedom to a slave was not just a matter of restoring dignity or social status, but fundamental humanity. It was a restoration of personal space – the right to self-chosen values and relationships, and hopefully also a place to call home.

Hobbes believed that, in the absence of law, humankind would descend into chaos, and life would become 'nasty, brutish and short'. He therefore saw the value of having a ruler who was to be given authority to maintain and enforce law and order over everyone within his or her jurisdiction. In this, his view was closer to the earlier dispensation, where rules were imposed from top down.

For John Locke, however, authority was to be established through the will of the people. A ruler is therefore answerable to parliament, which in turn represents – in theory, if not in practice – all citizens. Individuals were seen as equal and deserving of rights, each motivated by his or her own self-interest. Government and the law were established by consent and, by and large, were to interfere with people's individual freedoms as little as possible. That pattern established social atomism, the view that society is an aggregate of individuals who make it up. It has persisted to the present day, in spite of all the social changes and wars that have intervened over the centuries. It underlies debates about how much a government should or should not interfere in the lives of individual citizens.

At one extreme, totalitarian regimes have tried to control every aspect of an atomised society, at the other, government regulation is minimised. But in both cases, the structure of society is not organic, but comprises an atomised base of equal individuals, with a legal and political structure imposed over it. The question dividing the traditional left and right of political debate is the extent to which the aggregate base is seen as completely atomised, or as representing a compound entity called 'society'.

Here, for example, is the British Prime Minister Margaret Thatcher, speaking in 1987:

> And, you know, there is no such thing as society. There are individual men and women and there are families. And no governments can do anything except through people, and people must look to themselves first. It is our duty to look after ourselves and then, also, to look after our neighbours. There is no such thing as an entitlement, unless someone has first met an obligation.[41]

In an attempt to be fair, I have extended the quotation a little, rather than give just the first two sentences here, as is often the case, in order to show that, in her view, there was indeed some responsibility to help others, but only after looking after ourselves, and she goes on to speak about rights being balanced against responsibilities.

But notice the background assumption here. In a personalised world, as in my view of the network of human relationships as my plane descended over Europe, what comes to the fore is the essentially interconnected nature of society. Individuals have their place within it, and receive their identity from it. Removed from society, the individual is impoverished, and eventually becomes sub-human, deprived of language. But in this atomised view, individuals, with their own agenda and aspirations, their personal choices and freedoms, are the starting point. Social cohesion is to be maintained, because it is needed for survival, but only by light-touch regulation.

When this atomised view of society is extended into the sphere of economics, you have the phenomenon that is generally labelled 'neo-liberalism' – maximum freedom for the individual to pursue his or her own desired goals, with minimal tax and minimal intervention by government, beyond what is required to maintain law and order.

An atomised society, expressed in concrete?

I see this as the social and economic equivalent of the impersonal world revealed by science. We are essentially atoms in a void, collaborating practically and morally on the basis of enlightened self-interest. It is reflected in the twin poles of a broad western consensus about political and economic life – democracy and capitalism.

For many, those poles become the unquestioned good and the endpoint of any social or political journey. In *The End of History and the Last Man* the American economist Francis Fukuyama argued that the west had effectively ended any debate about the best way to organise society. Coming in 1992, just after the fall of the Berlin Wall and the disintegration of the Soviet Union, his judgement seemed unchallengeable.

Within political debate, there is a range of views, from individualistic liberalism on the one hand to more communitarian and socialist ideals on the other, and the balance of these is beyond our concern here. However, throughout that range, the justification of political action is generally based on the will of the people, whether real or

186

falsely invoked. Even those who wish to impose control from the top down at least pretend to justify their actions on the basis of an aggregate of individual needs. Things are done for the good of the people, even if the people do not necessarily appear to feel the benefit!

When, in an atomised society, people complain about their situation, the government response is to parade all the steps that they have already taken to provide what is needed. In effect, they say 'How can you possibly complain? We have invested millions of dollars or pounds in your area!' What they are less keen to ask is, 'Why has this existing expenditure not provided what you think you need?' And the reason they do not ask that question is because they fear the answer might be beyond their power to address.

In an atomised society, government tends to assume that every problem can be solved by an injection of cash or new legislation. It does not generally take into account the fact that, beyond the presenting problem, people's real complaint may relate to their collective loss of personal space, home and identity.

Most political issues are complex, and it would be pointless to attempt a simplistic analysis, but I would raise just one tentative question: is it possible that one component in a range of recent political phenomena – from Donald Trump's presidency, to the Brexit vote or the unrest in Hong Kong – may be a perceived loss of personal space and identity on the part of people who do not feel adequately represented?

For the purpose of examining the political implications of personal space, we need to take from this discussion one thing only: that the way in which most political decisions are justified is based on an atomisation of society, which is very different from the personalised and value-orientated perceptions and choices of individuals. Let us take an example from the Covid-19 pandemic. Rules about social distancing, imposed to minimise the spread of the virus, were justified by the aggregate need of society as a whole – we all benefit if transmission is stopped – but for individuals, their personal values and personal commitments may lead them to break the rules, not because they want to disobey on principle, but simply because their personal commitments override the potential benefit to society as a whole.

The ultimate horror: atomised lives, sacrificed at Verdun in 1916. The battle, in a process of mechanised slaughter unlike any before it, saw 377,000 French casualties and 337,000 German. Troops were thrown into battle in the hope that the sheer number of casualties they inflicted would eventually sap the other side of the strength or willingness to continue fighting. Yet each cross marks a personal tragedy and a family bereaved.

In an atomised society, people belong to classes or socio-economic groups. They are targeted by the media, based on their perceived shopping preferences, and are surveyed by those who want to know their net worth as consumers. In an atomised world, I represent a group, before I represent myself; I am expected to wear a social mask and act accordingly, and if I rebel, I am simply playing at being an eccentric and am therefore put in just another atomised pigeonhole.

From a capitalist point of view, it is easy to reduce people to an atomised role, as either a producer or consumer. The danger is that people may eventually come to see themselves in terms that are defined by their shopping. In an atomised world, democracy becomes the opportunity to manipulate the majority and then claim their mandate.

In such a society, companies that present themselves as 'global' are, of course, not concerned with global wellbeing at all; they create their own particular networks and spread them around the globe, which is quite another matter. Global capitalism is as narrowly focused in its loyalties as any local business empire, only more successful and widespread.

Atomisation thus promotes (or at least allows) rootlessness. You are seen as an individual with rights, but without taking into account your unique position and home. In an atomised world, the individual counts as one among millions, of infinitesimal value and influence. In a communitarian world, by contrast, the individual is part of a network, and his or her significance and value is given in terms of that larger but identifiable group.

Taken to its logical conclusion, social atomism might indeed have led to the global homelessness of which Heidegger warned. That it has not yet happened is down to another factor related to home.

NATIONALISM AND THE NEED FOR ROOTS

If, as individuals, our memory maintains our sense of self by holding together the values and experiences that form our personal maps, it is likely that a similar process maintains the' identity of groups, societies and nations. Just as an individual may answer the question 'who am I?' by considering different situations during his or her lifetime – from child at home, to school to parenthood and employment, to retirement – so a nation goes through historical episodes, some of which, at any one time, may become emblematic of its distinctive character.

History is not just a matter of events, but of the stories a nation tells itself about them.[42] Is British identity, for example, shaped by the Second World War, perhaps as seen through the prism of *Dad's Army*? Or by remembering its colonial period, as the hub of an empire? Or should England think of itself as a nation intimately linked with the rest of Europe, with English rule extending across Aquitaine? Or as a politically decapitated land, ruled by the Norman conquerors? Or as a set of kingdoms in a state of chaos, as Vikings and Saxons vie for control? Or as a far-flung province of the Roman Empire? Or as the most westerly part of the European mainland, connected by the land bridge extending across the Dover straits and the vast area of Doggerland before it became the North Sea?

History is an essential study, because history provides the narrative of national identity, putting our present situation into a broader perspective. But there are dangers in clinging to a sense of national identity. In the late nineteenth century, the British Empire exported standards of dress and behaviour to all corners of the globe, reinforcing, almost by caricature, what it meant to be British. But just as those who are fearful of ever leaving home, may fail to rise to the challenges of venturing into unfamiliar territory, so an attitude that elevates a particular idea of a national home above all others, may create a slippery slope towards localism, nationalism, prejudice and xenophobia.

Although it could become the very antithesis of the cosmopolitan dream, some sense of a national or local 'home' seems essential for individual or social well-being, and its loss can be devastating. So, for example, in her book *The Need for Roots*, Simone Weil, writing in exile from her native France during the Second World War, says:

> To be rooted is, perhaps, the most important and least recognised need of the human soul. It is one of the hardest to define. A human being has roots by virtue of his real, active and natural participation in the life of a community which preserves in living shape certain particular treasures of the past and certain particular expectations for the future … Every human being needs to have multiple roots. It is necessary for him to draw well-nigh the whole of his moral, intellectual and spiritual life by way of the environment of which he forms a natural part.[43]

190

And she grieves for her nation under occupation, and recognises the need for a politics that can provide for the wellbeing of the soul as well as the body.

Her concerns are not utilitarian but profoundly personal. She describes the sense of belonging and home experienced by the French. She notes how people who had previously thought of themselves primarily as from a particular Département, or region of France, were being drawn together, under occupation, to identify simply as French. This raises the fundamental question about how the various levels of commitment relate to one another. The level of nationhood is one of those, and the one that operates for political purposes, but it is certainly not the only one, nor necessarily always the most significant. Those who volunteered to fight for Britain in 1914, for example, were often sent into battle together as 'pals' from a particular city, so that their local commitment to one another as friends would reinforce their commitment as soldiers in a national struggle.

From the same post-war period, broader in scope and frightening in its implications, Hannah Arendt's *The Origins of Totalitarianism* explores ways in which groups of people may become isolated and stateless and therefore vulnerable to persecution. She shows how a sense of national identity may tend to subvert all other moral imperatives, isolating and distancing those who do not conform to a national or racial stereotype.

Nationalism is narrowness – a definition of home that sets itself apart from all other members of the species and other places on the planet. It largely ignores the interdependent nature of life. It tends to encourage force, rather than cooperation, as a means of establishing hegemony. It divides, and ultimately weakens people. It requires an ultimate commitment to a limited object. It turns the nation into a kind of deity – an abstract idea, superimposed upon a physical location. It tends to ignore the natural process of change.

Yet our fundamental need for a sense of home may create tribal loyalties: nationalism, racism, speciesism, or class or party affiliation. Our desire to know and affirm our identity and place in the world, may lead us to define ourselves over against others and to reject all that is foreign.

When there is a threat – as with a terrorist atrocity – a key feature of the response is for a community to come together and declare its solidarity. But, equally, those tempted to join a terrorist organisation may feel that their racial or religious identity is threatened, and therefore want to affirm themselves, even if that involves self-destruction, or the flouting of otherwise established norms of behaviour. Killing 'them' is a way of emphasising loyalty to 'us'.

Issues of home, nationality and identity, appear everywhere in politics. During the Brexit debates, for example, those in favour of remaining within the EU could point to the Enlightenment values shared across western democracies, of the need to forge economic and social links that make war between their nations impossible. They identified as Europeans, as well as British. At the same time, an emphasis on sovereign control and the right to trade globally on one's own terms, along with a fear that British identity was being eroded, weighed heavily on the other side of the debate. Neither position was exclusively rational, but both were explicable in terms of the need for personal space.

Sometimes, recognising the need for national identity and self-respect, however necessary and valid in itself, can have seriously negative consequences. This is revealed in what must surely count as one of the most disastrous political misjudgements made by any philosopher.

In a moment that was to colour the rest of his life, speaking to an audience gathered to celebrate his becoming the Rector of Freiburg University, the German philosopher Martin Heidegger attacked a fundamental principle of liberal education.[44] He argued that the role of the university was essentially a pragmatic and political one. It should not promote disinterested learning, but should equip students for their role in national development. The tragedy of his illiberal view lay in its context. In 1933, against a background of the rise of Hitler and National Socialism, it became clear that this ambitious academic was throwing his intellectual weight behind a political movement that, with the benefit of hindsight, we know was soon to descend into brutality and murder on an unprecedented scale. But why did he choose to do so? Did he not, even then, recognise its dangers?

This question has been discussed too many times already, and I have no intention of revisiting its many arguments, nor attempting to excuse Heidegger for his short-lived error.[45] But let us just consider Heidegger's feelings at that time, setting aside, for a moment, the fact that he was ambitious and persuasive, as well as stubborn and inflexible when confronted by uncomfortable truths later in life.

Heidegger had been brought up Catholic, in a family that was rooted in the small town of Messkirch in southern Germany – a 'home' to which he would return throughout his life, and where he was finally laid to rest. He was essentially a country boy, rooted in his local soil and proud of his national and local identity. Originally destined for the priesthood, he gave up theology and quickly established his talent for philosophy, but although intellectually brilliant, he remained suspicious of the sophisticated, cosmopolitan culture of university life.

During his first tenured appointment, at the University of Marburg, he established a cabin in the hills at Todtnauberg, to which he invited his students and where he delighted in wearing rustic clothes. He was an academic with the heart of a boy scout! His ability to hold a lecture hall spellbound led him to be nicknamed 'the magician of Messkirch', and yet he was more at home hiking in the mountains and sitting before a bonfire. He even admitted that the experience of the wind and of the countryside made his life at the university seem unreal.

A sense of home while walking through alpine meadows?

Proud and patriotic, he was devastated by the terrible birth of the Weimar Republic, with its mass unemployment and unaffordable war reparations imposed by the Treaty of Versailles. He wanted a sense of nationhood that was clean, decisive and unsophisticated.[46]

He was also torn between his student lover, Hannah Arendt – young, intellectual, and Jewish – who became his muse during the surge of creativity that leads to his first major work, *Being and Time*, and his home with his anti-semitic wife, Elfride, and two sons.

During the early 1930s you have, in Heidegger, a clash of identity, and therefore also of personal space. On the one hand, within the university, he has been an assistant to the phenomenologist Edmund Husserl, and a friend of the existentialist philosopher Karl Jaspers – a world that was cosmopolitan, sophisticated and partly Jewish. On the other, his roots were in Messkirch and up in his cabin; traditional, narrowly patriotic and countrified. Then, into that mix, comes Hitler, who – in his astonishing rise to power in 1933 –

promises decisive action to restore German national pride, to clear away the shambles of the Weimar Republic, to give direction and a sense of purpose to a nation that appeared to be drifting, lost, and in danger of a Communist takeover. That must have had a profound gut appeal to Hiedegger.

It didn't take him long to realise that National Socialism was not going to provide what he longed for, but by then the damage was done, and the academic world has been struggling to come to terms with him ever since. Clearly, Heidegger was one of the greatest thinkers of the twentieth century – both in his early existential phase, and in his later grasp of issues, such as the environment and the impact of technology – so how was it possible for such an intellect to be beguiled, however briefly, into supporting the Nazis, and in refusing later in life to repudiate his earlier views?

In my view, the answer lies precisely in the concept of 'home'. To the question 'where do you belong?' Heidegger was caught between the world of his success as a lecturer and academic, and his longing for the simple rural life. The experience of 'home' was always a key part of Heidegger's thinking, and in 1961 he returned to Messkirch to give a talk entitled 'Home', in which he reflected on the mystery of our origin, on death and on the churchyard, where he would eventually be buried.

In 1966, he finally accepted that his perception of the 1933 'National Awakening' as a Nietzschean 'will to power' was a 'great blunder'. Nevertheless, that blunder should be unsurprising, given his background and the philosophy he had developed in the previous decade. In *Being and Time* he points out that we do not choose our origins, but are 'thrown' into life with a particular set of circumstances; it is with these that we have to deal. He was thrown into a situation in which what he wanted for Germany was reflected in the propaganda claims of National Socialism. He wanted renewal and a sense of direction and purpose, and Hitler seemed to provide just that, reinforcing important elements in Heidegger's personal

195

space. Later in life, rather than directly repudiating National Socialism, he believed that Hitler had let him down. That makes little sense politically, but every sense in terms of his personal space. Hitler had offered but failed to deliver on his dreams of German renewal.

Heidegger refused to be associated with existentialist philosophy and was dismissive of Sartre, even though his writings had influenced the latter's thought. I suspect that was not based entirely on academic snobbery, but on a fundamental difference between Sartre and Heidegger. Sartre was, above all, a cultural aesthete, an academic and literary craftsman, one of the elite. Heidegger, for all his towering intellect, his magic on the lecture podium, and his commitment to serious, professional philosophy, was never that. He was a countryman from Messkirch, rooted in its blood and soil, and proud of it.

Leaving aside the Nazi overtones of that phrase, each one of us is rooted in 'blood and soil'; in the people and the places that have shaped us. We may acknowledge our roots or try to deny them, but only the former approach offers us the prospect of integrity and allows our sense of home to take on a political dimension. Heidegger's plight suggests that our political views are likely to be determined as much by our sense of 'home' as by reason or argument.

GETTING A BALANCE

Heidegger's fateful decision of 1933 may have been an extreme example, but it stands as a warning about an almost universal political dilemma lurking in our appreciation of personal space. It finds expression in racial and class tensions, in aggressive nationalism, in religious extremism and in the perceived threat of globalised industries. It flourishes in a political and spiritual vacuum, and is so widespread that its impact goes largely unexamined. It also undermines efforts to tackle the biggest single threat to humanity – climate change.

It is the dilemma of being torn between a nourishing and rooted localism on the one hand and the attraction of global and cosmopolitan principles on the other. Although it has political implications, it reflects the need for personal space, for a sense of belonging and for being understood and cared for rather than being excluded, marginalised or ignored. It is fundamental to appreciating human need in the political world of today.

Some benefits of a well-ordered society seem so obvious that they tend to be assumed rather than discussed. Beyond the provision of basic necessities, people are thought to need three things: freedom, the ability to pursue their own happiness and well-being, and growth.

But all three of these need to be held in check, rather than to be given free rein. Freedom is an unquestionable good. Those who have little or no freedom, are deprived of the possibility of living life to the full, reduced – literally or metaphorically – to slavery. Freedom should only be restricted, as the nineteenth century philosopher and politician J. S. Mill argued, in order to prevent people from harming others. At the other end of the scale, however, absolute freedom may lead to the paralysis of indecision, and with no restrictions on what I am able to do, my happiness is likely to be short-lived. So freedom cannot be an absolute good, but needs to be seen in the context of society.

Equally, every political system seems to be judged primarily on its ability to deliver goods and services. Economic benefits dominate discussions of national well-being – even among those whose judgements show subtle and historical sensitivity, such as Peter Frankopan.[47] His historical survey of the peoples living along the Silk Roads, re-shaping our view of the world, provides evidence that, when people are provided with a good standard of living and basic utilities, they will be satisfied and their society will remain stable. By contrast, deprivation feeds the desire for change and hence instability. That may be true, but is it the economic benefits themselves that provide stability, or something else? My hunch is that stability comes from the shared sense of purpose that a vibrant economy engenders.

But freedom and increased well-being require economic growth, which is probably the least challenged of the benefits offered – or at least promised – by government. On a biological level, growth helps us get to our maximum stature and to renew our tissues, but, once those two goals are reached, it needs to be restrained to prevent damage. Cell growth becomes cancerous if it breaks free from the body's control mechanisms and starts to invade surrounding tissue or colonise other organs. Indefinite growth, which might seem desirable from the perspective of the individual cell, would spell disaster for the body overall. Yet, when it comes to the economy, unlimited growth is seldom questioned as a goal. The secret of political success? It's the economy, stupid!

On a finite planet, we know that unconstrained growth will eventually lead to disaster. It did not seem so for those who originally saw growth through capitalism as a great motivator and a way of maximising resources, for it appeared as a blessing for all whose lives were blighted by lack of basic necessities. Within what was possible, even in the nineteenth century, there seemed little problem with growth. Of course, the industrial revolution spoiled large tracts of beautiful countryside and mined the earth for its resources, but the scale on which that was done, relative to the remaining resources, gave the impression that such growth could continue indefinitely. Up to the point at which basic necessities are satisfied, growth is a necessity for human survival. Beyond that point it becomes a choice, with consequences, both good and bad.

The problem is that material goods have largely become a substitute for personal satisfaction. If we are unsure of who we are, getting more stuff seems a reasonable, alternative goal. But this assumption is challenged by our sense of home, both as individuals and as a society. Sometimes, what is provided

198

locally offers a quality and satisfaction that is disproportionate to its material value.

In the 1970s, I worked for some years in a new town that had grown rapidly over a decade or so, as people had been relocated away from the deprived housing areas of the neighbouring city. Families established themselves in the newly provided workplaces and schools and later their elderly relatives joined them, often moving into blocks of four flats, built on the end of each row of terrace houses, so that they could live near their children and grandchildren. With the passing of years, however, many of the families moved away, but the elderly remained, isolated in their purpose-built accommodation. Some grieved for the loss of their old slums where they knew everyone and 'belonged'. They had everything provided for their comfort, but were utterly lost, victims of an atomised desire to help, but one that did not sufficiently appreciate the importance of their personal space.

Whether it's local town planning or a global threat, political thinking needs to strike a balance between two very different, but equally necessary tendencies:

On the one hand, the universal benefits of freedom, the provision of basic services, and growth, remain ideal in theory, but may leave a great deal to be desired in practice. Applied sensitively, they illustrate the dreams of liberal democratic societies. Applied ruthlessly, freedom becomes the first victim, and state control of goods and services can lead to misery, as Stalin proved in Soviet Russia. Globalised and generalised principles and goals, the stuff of political manifestos, when applied from the top down, need to be handled with care if they are not to threaten the localised identities that make life worthwhile.

On the other hand, local communities can provide support in ways that larger political organisations cannot. They operate at a level where personal space comes into its own. But localism, however richly beneficial in terms of supporting local shops, industries and people who might otherwise feel isolated, can also have its dangers. Localism can morph into nationalism and xenophobia, or can reinforce divisions between regions or between rich and poor. Personal space and a sense of home may underpin our commitment to those who share our own views, but they may also lead to the 'other' being objectivised, distanced, exploited or destroyed.

Layer upon layer – through locality, nationality, race or religion – we develop the overlays of our unique map. Taken together, they tell us who we are. But if we allow any one of them to become exclusive, we are in danger.

In this chapter we have contrasted two ways of looking at our interconnected world. One, leaning towards the global and cosmopolitan, promotes liberal views and broad political concepts, such as freedom and equality. It offers great scope for political idealism, but is always in danger – by its very insistence that all people should be considered equal – of promoting an impersonal social atomism. The other, leaning towards the national and the local, is deeply rooted in personal commitments. It promises the satisfaction of identity, solidarity and a sense of community and purpose. But it also threatens to divide the world into us and them, those who belong and those who are excluded and foreign.

One might be tempted, therefore, to go for universal ideals at the risk of social atomism, rather than fall into the narrowness of the nationalist or isolationist tendency. But that will never work, because it ignores the universal need for personal space and home.

We need to hold the two tendencies in balance, and accept that both have something valuable to contribute. But we need something else as well – a way of thinking about our home that is not politically divisive.

HOMELAND

The sense of being rooted in a locality was gently teased out in the German television series *Heimat*, which traced life of a small village from before the First World War until the latter part of the twentieth century. People come and go, but the life of the village continues; the passing of decades reflected in changes to the houses, transport, dress and work. Change takes place within an overall continuity that gives nostalgic comfort. We know we cannot avoid the former, but need to be assured of the latter. The essence of 'home' remains, even as generations are born and die.

British equivalents of *Heimat* might be *The Archers*, or *Coronation Street* – on-going sagas, so well established in the national consciousness that events they portray can sometimes invade the news as though they were real rather than scripted. In the USA, it could be the comforting familiarity of easy humour of *Friends*, or perhaps the homely portrayal of rural Minnesota in Garrison Keillor's broadcasts about life in the fictional *Lake Wobegon*.

To have a spiritual 'homeland' is an essential part of the human legacy, whether fought over, nurtured, or simply remembered from childhood. Those who have no natural home may try to re-create one, whether in terms of career, or religion, or friendships, or culture. Home is not an optional feature in our dreams of the good life.

The French philosopher and sociologist Henri Lefebure (1901–91) explored the symbols and experiences of everyday life, relating them both to the sense of alienation and to the positive way we are able to use social space. He argued that every society produces its special places, which act as symbols to express its activity.[48] He saw space as personal, social and political, reflecting the values and life-views of society, so that, if you want to reveal the presuppositions of society, you need to analyse the way it uses its spaces. Both for society as a whole and for the individual, the loss of personal space illustrates a loss of identity. Coming from a Marxist perspective, Lefebure was particularly concerned to warn that capitalism would invade the ordinary, shared life of society, turning it into a sphere for consumption on the one hand and the supply of services on the other.

So, given that the need to express a sense of home in our personal space is unavoidable, here is our question: is it possible to construct and use personal space in a way that avoids the traps of atomisation on the one hand and narrowly defined localism on the other?

This takes us beyond the scope of this book and into the realms of town and city planning and the attempt to create physical locations where people may live and work in an environment that attempts to provide for their personal, social, cultural and spiritual needs.

There have been plenty of examples of this from the early establishment of the 'garden city' as a more humane option to the 'concrete jungle' of urban life, through to the attempt to provide industry with a contented and stable workforce, pioneered by nineteenth century British industrial philanthropists such as the mill-owner Titus Salt, the Cadbury family and the Lever brothers. With the provision of good housing, schools, libraries and other social facilities, the communities of Saltaire, Bourneville and Port Sunlight, stand tribute to the attempt to enhance personal space in a way that helped rather than hindered economic production of wool, chocolate and soap. At no point were those communities other than the product of what might, perhaps unfairly, be described as enlightened self-interest, since the workers were totally dependent upon the largesse and approval of the industrialist owners. But at least they were an attempt to recognise that the establishment of a sense of community is an essential part of having a happy workforce. At the very least they did not regard their workers exclusively as atomised digits in a production process.

Recognising the need for home, it is not enough to see each person as a consumer, requiring a supply of shops, schools, sports facilities and the like. Those things should not simply appear in the costs column of the profit and loss ledger, but are the starting point for asking what 'the good life' can mean in the context of a domestic and working environment. Otherwise, we are left with a rather heartless 'neo-liberal' approach, where the profit-motive, minimum tax and minimum social provision becomes the norm.

The 'need' for austerity, or to balance the economic books, always masks other options. It would always be possible to increase the amount of tax gathered. To say that those of modest income should expect less help from society, is simply an alternative way of saying that those with greater wealth should contribute less. To say 'there is a limit to what is possible' is not to state a fact, but to impose a policy. As no doubt the good Titus Salt and his fellow philanthropists recognised, a narrowly selfish approach to social provision is self-defeating; largesse can also become profitable.

The rise of localism and nationalism shows just how much people are prepared to risk their economic well-being for the sake of maintaining their identity, to be acknowledged within their world. They want to be at the centre of a map of significance in which they have a unique part to play. They hate faceless bureaucrats, or legislation over which they have no control. This too is based on a sense of home. Those who complain that the world is not as kind or as generous as it was, seldom point to specific economic evidence, rather they have a sense that the world of their earlier years was more homely and acknowledging of their place within it.

However essential to our wellbeing, our sense of home is under constant threat. Populations have always been mobile, in the sense that they have shifted across the globe as refugees or economic migrants. For all but the Native Americans, the entire United States is comprised of the descendants of migrants. People travel to establish a new home: one that reflects their aspirations, or to live free from religious or political persecution or war. Doing so is never easy. They may elicit our sympathy, but may also be told to 'go back where they belong' by the unsympathetic defenders of their own national or local home. Their struggle is not merely for shelter and protection from harm, but for a personal space within which to establish themselves.

In this chapter, we have looked at the political extremes of personal space, contrasting a rootless cosmopolitanism with a blood and soil localism. At the risk of exaggeration, this gives focus to a fundamental political tension, which impacts at every level from the local workplace to international and global initiatives. Can our exploration of personal space give any clue to how it may be resolved?

My personal hunch – and it is perhaps no more than that – is that the answer lies with Hierocles' concentric circles. He does not deny that some things are closer and therefore more immediately important to us than others, so avoiding the utilitarian mistake of assuming that we can treat all alike. Neither does he fall for the alternative extreme and prioritise only what is close. Rather, he invites us to systematically shift our sphere of concern outwards through those concentric circles. In doing so, we retain the sense of home, along with its benefits of identity and meaning, but progressively extend that identity until it becomes global.

That leads us into our final challenge. If we are to effect any change in the world of personal space, playing our part in the interconnected human web that encloses the surface of our planet, then we will need to start by changing our own perception of home, engaging with it as the end point of our personal journey. How can we do this?

Chapter 9

Travelling Home

The journey of a thousand miles begins with a single step.
Lao Tzu[49]

The ancient Chinese proverb with which this chapter opens comes from the *Tao Te Jing*, the collection of teachings that forms the basis of Taoism, an appropriate tradition for our purposes because, unlike Confucianism, it opposes a rigid hierarchy by emphasising the natural, flexible and changing aspects of life. Travelling home will require both flexibility and determination.

Even if we set out intending to escape our present reality, the journey of self-discovery is likely to be circular. We may start from what we now think of as home, but, in a broader sense, home is also our destination. As we travel, we re-shape our personal map, adding to it new experiences and re-assessing old ones, but our destination, however vague, will be sensed as the place where we belong, and thus also our home.

So far, we have used the image of a map to convey the way in which we give our world value and meaning, but a map is only useful if we are prepared to use it as a guide for our journey.

THE JOURNEY

The narrative of a journey has been one of the most popular and profound of all literary forms, from Homer to Tolkien, and literature can help us to put imaginative flesh on the bones of a philosophy of personal space.

Whether as a quest, an adventure, or an inner process of self-discovery, journeys highlight life's transitions and compulsions: growing into adulthood; establishing a new relationship or recovering from a failed one; pursuing a new career, a lover or a white whale; negotiating a mid-life crisis; gradually coming to accept old age and death. Life may be described in terms of a journey, with a new sense of home as the end of its narrative arc.

In Virgil's *Aeneid*, for example, the narrative opens mid-journey, as the Trojans, driven by fate and nearly thwarted by shipwreck and love, head for the Italian shore. The drama of the epic poem makes exactly the point explained in Heidegger's rather more mundane prose, namely, that we find ourselves thrown into life in a particular set of circumstances and are thereafter forced by them to make the choices that shape our lives.

Even without the help of fate, love or a storm, we may nevertheless be impelled to start out on a journey by inner impulse or external challenge. We may, with Laurie Lee, set out one midsummer morning, hardly pausing to look back at our mother, working by our childhood home in its west-country village, as we embark on our new life. Or, with Frodo Baggins, we may find ourselves leaving the comfortable security of The Shire in Tolkein's *Lord of the Rings*, with some trepidation, fearful of what may lie ahead.

206

Leaving home at the beginning of the journey marks the point at which the hero or heroine feels compelled to engage with their quest. It may be to return home to Ithaca, to found Rome, to destroy a ring in the fires of Mordor, or simply to discover one's own authentic self, freed from the masks of convention.

In *The Wizard of Oz*, Dorothy leaves a drab Kansas to find her dream world. But at any time, since this is a dream, she is able to return home simply by clicking her heels together. The story juxtaposes fantasy and reality, the longed-for 'home' of self-discovery with the reality of a physically located 'home' with all its limitations. When she finally returns to Auntie Em, Dorothy declares, 'There's no place like home!' But is that really an affirmation of the same place from which she started, or the result of the new perspective that only travel can bring?

Sometimes I despair of philosophy, for its rational arguments scarcely do justice to the more subtle nuances of human experience. So much more can be revealed in poetry, as when, in the wonderful final section of 'Little Gidding', the fourth of T. S. Eliot's *Four Quartets*, he says:

> We shall not cease from exploration
> And the end of all our exploring
> Will be to arrive where we started
> And know the place for the first time.

Eliot quotes from Lady Julian of Norwich, a fifteenth century English mystic, that 'all shall be well, and all manner of thing shall be well.' Reaching back to a fixed point, where the fragility of the world rests in something reassuringly permanent, Eliot echoes the mystic's vision of everything that is made being as small as a hazelnut in her hand, and marvelling that something so insubstantial does not simply vanish. So there it is, our home, our personal *axis mundi*, the centre of our world, the end of our journey, the place for which we long, and in which we can at last be truly ourselves.

And yet its nature remains as fleeting and insubstantial as the hazelnut in the palm of her hand.

Sometimes a journey is driven by the power of observation, so that the very ordinariness of each place or incident becomes special. In *Ulysses*, James Joyce's homage to Dublin, we wander through the city and observe the ordinary lives of its people. Bloom's wanderings of 16 June 1904 are a journey through all the personalised space of Dublin, revealing its character and thereby making the city itself a home.

Exiles remember a home to which they hope, one day, to return; never more poignantly expressed than in the psalm:

> By the waters of Babylon, we sat down and wept when we remembered thee, O Zion.[50]

But Zion was not as they remembered it, and on their return to Jerusalem, the temple had to be re-built. We may know the familiar place for the first time on our return, but only because our travels or exile have given it a new perspective. Would it have been the same if we had stayed?

We may dream of finding a perfect place, whether over the sea or over a rainbow, where we shall finally and definitively be 'home'. But for most people, most of the time, that remains a dream, as they deal with the practicalities of the journey and moving on. 'Birds have their nests ... but the Son of Man has nowhere to lay his head.' So said Jesus, as he journeyed inexorably towards Jerusalem and death.

Sometimes thoughts and ideas are woven into a travel narrative. Robert M. Pirsig's *Zen and the Art of Motorcycle Maintenance*, sets philosophical reflections in the context of a journey by motorbike across the USA. The physical journey, and the relationship between father and son, mirrors the intellectual quest for quality in life, a sense of what is worthwhile, and – in doing so – a sense of fundamental values and of home.

Equally, in another narrative journey, Chaucer's *Canterbury Tales* has the pilgrims share their stories, secular and bawdy though some may be, in the context of a pilgrimage, a journey with a spiritual goal, designed to encourage personal reflection or penance. The overall impact, as in so many narratives that embody a journey, is that we go along together, learning from the great variety of experiences along the way, and from those with whom we travel. There will be adventures along the way. Bunyan's *Pilgrim's Progress*, spells out each in graphic imagery to create an overall allegory of life as a spiritual journey.

Notice the common feature of all these literary journeys and the reason they have such value. They present us with *the mapping of personal space by their authors*. They do not show life in an impersonal, empirically verifiable way, but life as we encounter and interpret it – or rather, as their authors intended us to interpret it. These narratives are shot through with meaning, value and direction.

The theme of a journey, far from being limited to the classics, influences all fiction, including the most popular.

THE FICTION OF LIFE

Pick up almost any work of popular fiction, or – if you prefer to have the process spelled out for you – any of the books that claim to help you write your first bestselling novel, and you will find the narrative shape quite predictable. Starting with a question, a trauma, a challenge or an impending threat, the story moves on to describe how the principal character responds. He or she has a journey that will almost certainly involve false starts and obstacles to be overcome, with a final climax of frustration as the hoped-for goal is thwarted at the last minute. But then, at the end, all is resolved. If romance is your thing, they finally discover that they are deeply in love; if it's a detective story, the culprit is revealed.

Not all fiction takes that form, of course. A book may be challenging, or experimental. Its language may be amazing, but without any discernible sense of narrative, in which case you are probably in the deeper recesses of literary fiction. Or you may find yourself turning the pages slower and slower, as you luxuriate in the prose, rather than becoming engaged with the plot. But, for now, let's stick with the page-turner.

What is the on-going attraction of the murder mystery format? Clearly, in real life, things are never that straightforward and the murderer will probably never be found. But the reassurance given by the traditional structure is that it provides exactly that – structure. We know, as we watch or read, that there is a definitive answer to the question about who committed the murder, and that it will eventually be revealed. The narrative journey, however intricate its twists and turns, ends with a sense of home.

That is also the appeal of traditional religious, humanist and Marxist narratives. They offered a direction, a goal and a future certainty – whether it is the final judgement of Christ, the progress of enlightened humanity, or the dictatorship of the proletariat. They provide ready-made global maps, over which our own personal maps can be laid.

Imagine sitting down to plot out a work of fiction – whether it is a play, a short story or a novel. You arrange a cast of characters, giving each a 'home' in their backstory. Where do they live? Where do they belong? What values do they hold? What are their hopes and fears? Then, having assembled your characters, you could attempt to slot them into your pre-designed plot. However, many would argue that the best fiction is not plotted out in that way. Rather, it starts with a conflict into which the characters are pitched, and allows the narrative to develop naturally, as they interact with one another. What might that suggest? Simply, that each character has his or her personal map, and that, as they interact, their maps fuse into an overall story.

We have already shifted the most basic question from 'who are you?' to 'where do you belong?' Now we shift it again, to 'where is your life going?' Home is both the starting point and end of every journey. Without a sense of home, one is simply wandering aimlessly, perhaps cursed to do so forever.

The image of the journey fits neatly with the process of mental mapping, because we are not totally determined by our backstory; we are living, changing beings, shaping ourselves by our decisions and being shaped by our circumstances. And each of those decisions and circumstances finds its place within the maps that we are drawing all the time within our neural pathways. We should not take this too literally, of course, for it is impossible to see the way our brain actually patterns things out, but through recognition and memory, value and response, we know that the end result is the map that records our journey.

If you want to know who I am, you must allow me to tell you my story, for it is in the story that I reveal my journey, and in the journey that I reveal my home, the place where I am most truly myself.

Sometimes narratives are not enough, and the sense of home eludes our conceptual or imaginative grasp. When it does, we may find it helpful to use a medium that goes beyond words – music.

MUSICAL INTUITIONS OF HOME

Both popular and religious music is full of references to journeys and to home. From 'country roads, lead me home, to the place where I belong …' or 'by the time I get to Phoenix' to the nostalgic yearning for Strawberry Fair and for the girl who 'once was a true love of mine'. Or from the Beatles 'she's leaving' for the girl finally escaping the confines of home, to the sentimental 'there's no place like home', or even the sweet chariot that is 'coming for to carry me home'.

We shudder at the curse of the Flying Dutchman, forever sailing his ghostly ship into the opening bars of Wagner's opera, or are lifted to an aching climax of longing in the *in paradisum* of every requiem mass, but perhaps especially in Fauré's haunting treble line.

It is the vocation of the artist, writer and musician, to translate the impulses of our immediate experience into something deeper and richer – a narrative, or an image, or a sequence of sound that evokes a sense of meaning. We respond, but cannot always explain why. We hear the music and feel ourselves caught up in something that gives us a sense of wholeness, a challenge, or a meaning that we cannot put into words. Like the insights of the drinker, lost in subsequent sobriety, the moments when music gives a tingle of profound awareness, can seldom be given a logical or cash value on later reflection.

Music influences the emotions, stirs memories, evokes relationships and locations, provokes aggression or invites relaxation. It speaks of things that cannot be described literally; it evokes insights that cannot be explained.

Changing musical styles reflect the developments of our sense of personal space. In the shift in music from the Baroque, through the Classical to the Romantic, structure and order give way to a more flexible style, expressing emotions rather than the pleasure of patterns. Patterns remain, of course, but they are the undertow of a swelling emotional musical line. Sometimes it is just a hint or a single note that sends tingles down the spine. In the Saint-saëns organ symphony, there is a moment when the organ gradually inserts itself below the melody, a deep almost unnoticed note that then swells, finally bursting in a chord of magnificent and overwhelming power; a chord that fires off the orchestra in a headlong dash towards the climax of the piece. At that point, you don't need to attend carefully; you can simply relax back and allow the emotional power of the music wash over you.

And yet, with all music, there is the sense of order, the repeated rhythm, the inevitable closing of a phrase, or the gentle but persistent building of one, as practiced so perfectly by Sibelius. There is, in the symphonic work of the Romantic or later periods, a balance between structure and a musical painting of the emotions.

Swelling chords perfectly express the tumult of human emotion – we can become immersed in the power of Mahler or fired up by the rushing power of Shostakovich's fifth symphony. There are also moments when the natural and the emotional blend – as with *The Lark Ascending* by Vaughan Williams. In imitating the song of the lark it also expresses the soaring ambition of the soul (that old-fashioned word!). We sense the violin and bird circling upwards into a perfection that is heaven, death, orgasm, or all three at once.

Music speeds us up or slows us down: the gentle flow of new-age therapeutic music, the the brassy challenge of a march, or the constant rhythmic pulse of a disco. Music creates a map of sound that overwhelms and catches us up into something inexpressible. At the end of a great piece of music, its truth remains unspoken, because its language is untranslatable. It 'says' something to us; it hints of the map as yet unrecognised or undeveloped; it reminds us of something still beyond recall – a 'yes' to that to which we cannot give a name.

I remember singing Verdi's Requiem in St Paul's Cathedral, London, when I was a student. When the brass section heralded the *Dies Irae*, the sound echoed around the great dome, immediately above the heads of the choir. I doubt I was the only person there whose spine was tingling, and a conviction of meaning – even for the cynic that I had half-become – infused the space around us. Here was an inescapable truth, but one that was beyond explanation.

Could we call it 'the music of the spheres'? It's impossible now to get back to the intellectual place where such ideas could be entertained. We know there are no glassy spheres above us. But that does not stop the tingling or the awareness. We touch reality here, even if words and concepts fail to grasp it. We also sense, but cannot demonstrate, that in that

213

moment of tingle we feel both insignificant and authentic. We are where we belong, even if our arriving throws the rest of life into a confusion of irrelevance.

Music is therapy for those who are lost, nostalgia for the outcasts, comfort for those whose home is threatened, strength for those in despair. Music stirs patriotism, speaks of a home, whether a village, town, nation or religious certainty. Music touches the sense of home and makes it real. Those who listen or perform, in losing themselves in the music, also find themselves at home.

Both narratives of journeys and the emotions generated by music can offer us a starting point for our own journey home.

CULTIVATING OUR PERSONAL SPACE

Many of the observations and arguments in this book refer – directly or indirectly – to religion. This is inevitable, for a majority of people throughout the centuries have expressed their sense of meaning and purpose through religion. It is also true that, without the conventional mapping offered by religion, some people feel adrift, sensing the loss of horizon and the 'breath of empty space'. But not all. The experience of meaning and purpose, with the sense of belonging and of home, is not limited to the conventionally religious. As we have seen, it is equally generated within aesthetic experience. We are moved, challenged and confronted by art – whether it is in the visual arts, music or literature. Art reminds us of who we are, and of where we stand. We are given direction and impelled forward, and that is true both of created works of art and of the aesthetic sense of wonder that we find as we contemplate nature.

So we should not think of the quest for home as essentially religious, unless we are prepared to accept that the sensitive appreciation of nature and of the aesthetic is also religious. Home is for everyone, and we may cultivate it in whatever way we find appropriate.

214

How might we do so?

In 1996, the American anthropologist Keith Basso, produced a study of the Apache and their way of looking at their landscape in a book entitled *Wisdom Sits in Places*. Journeying from place to place, the Apache would give each a name that reflected its character, gradually constructing a social and cultural map of their territory. In other words, to use his term, they were doing 'retrospective world building' – shaping an already existing landscape and giving it meaning, making it their home. In doing this, he says 'we are, in a sense, the place-worlds we imagine'. In practical terms, when it comes to cultivating a sense of home, we can learn a great deal from this Apache tradition.

Imagine, like the Apache, walking through your personal world – its places, its people, its groups, its ideas – and naming each part of it intentionally: this is the place where ... the person who ... the group within which I ... the idea which led me to ... Such a world, however transient, has the quality of home.

Then add the dimension of time. Where did I start out? What has been my journey? What maps have sustained me? These questions, reflecting the archaeology of our internalised mapping system, are the basis of a kind of personal spirituality that requires no religious commitment, but which touches on the very deepest part of ourselves.

My suggestion is that we do not need new ideas of experience to establish a sense of home, merely a willingness to look around, pause, reflect and – just for a moment – hold on to the significance for us of what we are looking at or thinking about, allowing it to be 'placed' within our world. That process requires no special techniques, although it can be enhanced, as we shall see a little later.

However, there is one aspect of this process of cultivating our personal space that is reflected most obviously in religion: the energy and enthusiasm of new converts. It is not that they

215

suddenly gain an intellectual understanding of all the beliefs and doctrines of the group to which they now belong – many over-zealous converts need to be restrained from promoting what might be seen as a simplistic ideology. No; the burst of energy that comes with conversion is more a matter of feeling liberated by being accepted, 'welcomed home' and being given a new map within which things appear to take their natural place.

What follows from this observation, however, is that many of us, for much of the time, exhibit the frustration of half-belonging, being half-engaged and expecting to be no more than half-accepted. Whether it is in a relationship, or in an act of creativity – writing, painting, acting, or whatever – there is a huge difference between those who walk through the part they are given, either with a nervous sense of dislocation, as though waiting to be found out as a phoney, or the bored indifference of one who has seen it all before, and those who throw themselves into it without reservation.

So the process of cultivating our personal space requires three things: observation, reflection and commitment. If any one of those is missing, we are likely to drift. But there are also hazards that we need to avoid.

THE DANGER OF NOSTALGIA

Beware the backward glance. The original meaning of the Greek term 'nostalgia' was 'longing for home' used of soldiers who were fighting in far flung places and feeling cut off from their roots. Today it refers to a longing for an idealised past. But we only feel nostalgic for the past if, in some way, we feel that we belong there or were content there. Nobody is going to feel nostalgic for a past in which they were oppressed, abused or lost.

At one time I had a caravan, in which I used to stay for three nights every week to save a long commute to work. Arriving back at the van after a day in the office, especially in the summer months, I'd find myself surrounded by holidaymakers preparing their barbecues beneath the trees. It was a good arrangement. Then, one morning at work, I received a call from the campsite owner; my van had been stolen.

I left the office immediately, jumped into the car and returned to the site. It was weird. The power line still snaked across the grass to the hook-up, and the steps up to the door were exactly where they always had been. The tank for water was still in place – since this was long before one could get services piped direct into your RV or caravan – but its pipe had been disconnected and lay on the grass. But the van itself had gone, as though beamed upwards, leaving its surroundings intact.

Then it started to dawn on me that all my personal effects and clothes had also gone, my books, my familiar mugs and glasses, the magazine I had left on the table, open at the article I'd started over breakfast. All gone. And over the next few days and weeks, I kept remembering things that were no longer available to me. It was a kind of bereavement; my 'home', for at least part of each week, was no longer there.

For a week or so I wallowed in nostalgia, convinced that I could never replace what had been lost. Then I pulled myself together, bought a new van, and re-stocked my temporary home.

The old van may have suited me well, but it was never perfect and it would not have been a permanent feature of my life, for, after a year or two, my work relocated to central London and I was on the move again. The problem with nostalgia is that it tries to stop the process of change. It locates our future in the past, the one place we can never be. It is also as selective as our memory.

Nostalgia can lead to regret, which, if left unchecked, may sap the energy required to learn and move on. If the most important features of our personal space are in the past, we have some serious thinking to do. We cannot reverse time, cannot become again what once we were, and if we did

217

succeed in returning to our past home, it would anyway have changed while we were away.

The process of travelling home may require us to reflect on our past, but that does not mean we should be constantly looking back. As we move through life, homes inevitably get shed along the way. Things, careers, people and places that dominated our world at one time, gradually fade out of significance. Finding and cherishing our sense of home is a creative process that links past and future. We learn from where we have been, but also from our hopes and aspirations.

Nostalgia is like a trampoline. If you crawl on to it and try to stand still, you will achieve nothing more than a feeling of unsteady queasiness. If you pluck up courage and leap on to it, it may enable you to bounce higher than you had expected.

A word of caution. If meditation and eastern philosophy has a contribution to make here, it is that our life is impoverished if it is lived entirely in the past and the future. Neither is real, in the sense that neither presently exists; its reality is limited to our memories and our hopes. We need to consider the reality of our personal space in the present moment.

HOME IN THE PRESENT

In Buddhist philosophy, all things are interconnected and liable to change. Nothing has a fixed essence, because everything is in a state of flux. This is based on the observation that everything arises in dependence upon causes and conditions, and will cease once they no longer operate. In reality, everything is *shunyata*, emptiness, without inherent existence. That is not a negative comment, but a positive one; everything exists in an ever-changing present.

Therefore, from a Buddhist perspective, it is inadequate to think of myself as a separate entity, looking 'out' upon the world; rather, I am an ever-changing part of that world. If we fail to recognise this, it is argued, we are liable to crave and cling to ideas, people, things, hoping that we may thereby keep them forever. But that way lies suffering, because we are trying to do the impossible. Our sense of home therefore needs to be a present experience, and – like everything else – it needs to be open to change.

Home is everywhere and home is within us. It is the present reality, rather than a future destination or a nostalgic glance back to childhood. I am reminded of a quote from the Buddhist author Thich Nhat Hanh:

> My path is the path of stopping, the path of enjoying the present moment. It is a path where every step brings me back to my true home. It is a path that leads nowhere. I am on my way home. I arrive at every step.

Home is an experience of belonging and being centred. It is not an external location, but a sense of place; not something to be discovered, but to be cultivated.

However corny or glib it may sound, it remains true that the secret of life for a Buddhist is that life has no secret. The clue to the mystery of the universe is that the universe has no mystery. To speak of mystery implies concealment, waiting to be revealed only when the right idea or person or theory comes along. In fact, the world lies all before us; its reality is that within which we live, move and have our being.

That clarity of present experience is offered by the many forms of mindfulness practice, whether Buddhist or secular. One of the most common is the mindfulness of breathing.

We sit in silence and time has vanished. We have been counting our breaths, focusing on the passing of air in and out of the nostrils, or the chest rising and falling. I become aware, of the cushion beneath me, of my hands gently resting on my lap, palms upturned, thumbs lightly touching. And now I stop counting, but continue to be aware of each breath. I am held, suspended, comfortably floating, strangely aware of every part of the body, but with no idea of its size. I could be huge or minute, expanding upwards, or just held as if capable of floating away. There is no separation between self and other. While I sit, I am utterly at home.

I sit perched on the present moment; just watching as thoughts and feelings appear and disappear. It's like surfing a wave, poised and tipping forward, still but moving, always on the verge of a headlong plunge that never comes.

If the mindfulness of breathing enables us to engage with the present moment, a mediation of *metta*, or loving kindness, uses the mapping of our personal space. Traditionally, it works through the same concentric circles we saw outlined by the Stoic philosopher Hierocles. Emotional engagement with wishing well starts with the self and works outwards, to embrace a good friend, a neutral person and even someone we find difficult. At each point we imaginatively expand our circle of concern and good will. Finally, it is spread outwards to all living creatures.

Meditation may not be for everybody, but I think it provides a good model for the process of observation, reflection and engagement that brings our personal space, and therefore our home, into focus. Just as an intimate relationship is maintained and enhanced by constant acts of attention, so our personal space needs to be given the benefit of regular attention if we are not to drift through life.

There is another teaching from the Buddhist tradition that may help us as we make our journey. The starting point of the Buddhist path is the observation that life is never quite what we hoped it would be; it is flawed, limited and unsatisfactory. That is not a negative interpretation, simply a fact of life for finite, transient beings in our kind of world. The Buddha taught that the root cause of human suffering was the attempt to grasp and hold on to what we want, desperate to prevent it from changing, or craving for things to be different. To avoid emotional suffering, we need to be realistic. This is not a matter of passively accepting whatever life brings, but –

as in the Stoic tradition – of knowing what things we have within our power to change and what things we do not.

This can apply to our concept of home. We may be tempted to grasp and hold on to a particular notion of home – perhaps in terms of a person without whom we cannot live, or a place, or a career, or a level of wealth, or status without which we feel life would be intolerable. Rather than allowing our mapped personal space to show the way towards our home, we are tempted to define and fix a home and then impose it on ourselves and the rest of our world.

The result can lead a person to be described as single minded, or determined, or stubborn, or a fanatic for the cause, or unquestioningly committed to a religion, a political system, a nation, a race or whatever. That is unlikely to bring that person satisfaction, and it makes life increasingly difficult for other people, especially if they question that chosen definition of home.

We should therefore try to avoid grasping at our idea of home, for it will change, along with everything else in the world. There is no point in trying to freeze it in a moment of time – either in the nostalgic past or the future of our craved future success. Home emerges from the points of value on our personal map; it is not an external goal to be imposed upon them. Our enjoyment of home needs to incorporate an element of letting go, however much we love it. We need to reflect on and seek to enhance our homes, but without getting too restrictive. Our nest will one day become an empty nest. Can we live with that? Can we make the necessary adjustments?

Everyone will find his or her own way of developing a sense of home, and what works best will depend on part of the sequence in which we engage with the process of thinking about personal space, engaging with it, and building within it.

OBSERVE AND THINK FIRST

Earlier in this book we examined Martin Heidegger's exploration of personal space and home in his article 'Building, Dwelling, Thinking'. I think he got it wrong, not in the arguments he used, but in the order of words in his title. I think it should have been 'Thinking, Dwelling, Building'.

To appreciate who we are and where we belong, we first need to stop, observe and think – to survey the trajectory of our lives, with their high and low points, their dreams and fears, successes and failures. We also need to think realistically about the world within which we live, the fragility of human life and the vastness of space. It is that initial process of observing and thinking that this book is aimed to encourage.

Only once that basic work is done, can we expect to be more aware of our personal space, and therefore more ready to 'dwell' in the sense of being committed to the place, people and the ideas we call 'home'. To commit first and think afterwards is a recipe for disappointment or narrow fanaticism.

And only once that commitment is made, does it make sense to build, or move, or re-decorate, or buy that caravan, or re-locate to be nearer family and friends, or change career, or change partner, or seek relationship counselling, or jack it all in and travel the world. My hunch, not entirely free from the promptings of my own experience, is that many of us make the mistake of starting with that last stage and walking backwards. Unsure of who we are or where we belong, we assume that all will become clearer once we move house, change career or find a different partner.

We cannot escape from the map references that have been contributed by all our previous homes, but – if human freedom and creativity mean anything – there is always a chance that we can shape or enhance our future personal space, building the 'home' that makes us who we are.

GARDENING AND CLEANING

This book has largely been about ideas; about why we need a sense of home, and what part it plays in shaping our identity. But ideas are of little use if they do not lead to practical action. So, in spite of the sequence suggested in the last section, there will be times when gestures of commitment enable us to experience more clearly what we feel and where we belong.

From secular therapists and lifestyle gurus to Buddhist monks, there is no shortage of people who will argue persuasively that, by cleaning your home, tidying away or disposing of all your clutter, simplifying your needs and creating an environment of pristine minimalism, you will also be clearing your mind.

It is true that an improved environment and simplified lifestyle may help to de-clutter our mind, but it is not a necessary or universal truth. There are people who are content and maintain clarity of mind and purpose even when picking their way round the most confused and over-stocked of domestic settings. I think of the old couple who introduced my younger self to music and literature, tucked away in their tiny cultural nest, overloaded with books and records. For them de-cluttering would have been absolutely wrong; their setting was exactly what they needed. The Scandinavian approach to clean space is not for everyone, especially if it is not supplemented by a sauna and a good dose of hygge!

However, even if it is not a guaranteed way to establish a sense of home, cleaning and gardening have an important part to play in becoming aware of our personal space. Until we start to clean and care for somewhere, it cannot become our home. Even if you have lived in a house for decades, you are only a lodger if you have not, in some way, cared for it and set your stamp upon it.

Cleaning and tidying are not just means to an end, but an end in themselves. It is not the tiny pieces of gravel that benefit when the monk rakes that garden in that Zen temple in

Kyoto. The act of raking, making the stone look like flowing water, is itself a spiritual practice.

I am hopeless as a gardener, and certainly cannot be trusted to distinguish between weeds and treasured plants in a well-stocked bed. But the simple act of trimming a hedge and cutting a lawn, generates a sense of belonging that I cannot achieve by sitting at my computer looking out upon the garden. The fact that 'building' comes last in my three-stage process of enhancing our personal space, does not imply that it can be neglected. Our home is not some future state, in which we can start to build only once we have established who we are. It is an on-going process, in which, at every point, something of the building element is vital. If it were not so, few would travel hopefully to the garden centre or furniture store.

Sometimes it takes a bit of practical action to kick-start our thinking about our personal space, and it is unlikely that our home will ever be established without it. And that applies as much to the other features of our personal space and identity as to the physical place where we live. If you aspire to be a writer, just get to the keyboard and do it; if a photographer, get your camera out; if a dancer, risk taking to the floor. Dreams lurking in the corners of our personal space, need to be addressed practically, if only to show them to be unrealistic. We become something new only after we have discovered whether our aspirations are serious possibilities or fantasies.

COMING OUT OF THE CINEMA

There is a moment when you read the last paragraph, close the book and look up into your recently familiar room. Or perhaps it is when you stand and make your way towards the exit of the theatre or concert hall, still half engaged with the play or music. But for me, it is particularly when I step out of the cinema into the evening traffic, taking in the sudden coolness, noise and pace, but with my emotions still engaged with the film I have been watching.

In that moment, however fleeting, the world seems different. It is as though you are remembering something long since forgotten, or a task left unfulfilled. You are almost sad to be back to the normality of city life, fumbling in your pockets for gloves and scarf. Asked whether you want to join others for a drink or meal, you are – just for that moment – not quite sure of anything.

It may last for no more than a few seconds, but at that point you are looking at the world in front of you through someone else's eyes. You have, for the last hour or so, been immersed in someone else's map, engaged with their personal space. You see things using their coordinates of value; you have adopted their home. Now, suddenly, you have returned to the familiar street you left what seems like an age ago.

The familiar re-asserts itself quickly; you know how to respond to the friendly question about having a drink, where you live and where you parked the car. You have clicked back into your own personal space. But, every once in a while, the experience sticks, and the map within which you have been temporarily engaged is nested within your own; it becomes something you reflect on, and something that may just serve as a pointer on your journey home.

All culture – whether a book, piece of music, play, film or religious ceremony – is the opportunity to borrow its creator's personal space and thereby to see the world through his or her eyes. At its best, we can learn from that borrowing and make some of its elements our own.

FRIENDS IN OUR PERSONAL SPACE
Reflecting on my own personal space, one thing becomes overwhelmingly clear: friends and family occupy all the most important places on the map. There are plenty of other things

that draw my attention and invite my commitment, but none has the power of friendship.

Even after years of separation, meeting a friend has the quality of arriving home. I sense immediately that they have retained their place within my personal space and have continued to be part of me, remotely shaping my views and values, even by their unremembered presence.

In a society that is so easily atomised – where we slip into becoming consumers, punters, members or voters, rather than individuals – friendship enables us to remain human. It has been explored by philosophers and writers over the years, including, recently, Mark Vernon[51], and cherished within the world's religions. Friendship creates a sense of home that can override our social and political commitments, a point made succinctly by that quintessentially Enlightenment figure, Voltaire …

'L'amitié est la patrie' (Friendship is our homeland)

There's nothing like sharing a joke with an old friend!

Our personal space is constantly changing, and its changes are the waymarks along our journey home. Shaping our maps and engaging with our journey is a natural process, but it need not be a solitary one. We learn from one another, as we glimpse maps other than our own.

It seems to me that the goal of much therapy, and the general aim of the good life, is to allow us to live with a natural sense of integrity; to act in ways that pull together both the particularity of the place in which we find ourselves, and the aspirations and values we cultivate. We aspire to know who we are, because we know both where we are from and where we wish to go. That is the benefit of coming to terms with our personal space, and it pulls together the wisdom of religion, philosophy and psychology, melding the three disciplines into a single goal: to be 'at home'.

Nothing remains forever; our homes will come and go as, within the maps of our personal space, people and ideas vie for our attention. And, for many, life will be touched by the tragedy of homelessness and loss; with them we grieve. All life involves suffering and some degree of homelessness, for it is never exactly what we imagined it would be.

But that should not detract from our on-going quest to shape our personal space and cultivate a sense of home within whatever circumstances life throws at us, so that we are able to say honestly and with conviction 'This is where I belong!'

...

Bibliography

Many books have been referred to directly in the text, and their authors are listed in the Index of Names. In addition, I have found the following of particular interest:

Bachelard, Gaston *The Poetics of Space*, 1961

de Certeau, Michel *The Practice of Everyday Life*, University of California Press, 1984

Eliade, Mircea, *The Sacred and the Profane*, 1956 (English edition 1959)

van Fraassen, Bas C, *An Introduction to the Philosophy of Time and Space*, Columbia, 1985.

Gorner, Paul *Heidegger's Being and Time: an introduction*, CUP, 2007

Hall, Edward T., *The Hidden Dimension*, Anchor Books, 1969

Jaynes, Julian *The Origin of Consciousness in the Breakdown of the Bicameral Mind*, 1976

Lefebure, Henri *The Production of Space*, Blackwell, 1974 (English translation, 1991)

McGilchrist, Iain *The Master and his Emissary*, Yale, 2010, expanded edition 2018.

Merleau-Ponty, Maurice *Phenomenology of Perception*

Paden, William E. *Religious Worlds*, Beacon Press, 1988.

Palissot, Charles *Les Philosophes*, edited by Jessica Goodman and Olivier Ferret, and translated into English as *The Philosophes*, Open Book Publishers, 2021

Patterson, George *The Later Heidegger*, Routledge, 2000

Quill, Lawrence *Liberty after Liberalism*, Palgrave Macmillan, 2006.

Safranski, Rüdiger *Martin Heidegger: Between Good and Evil*, Harvard UP, 1998.

Smart, Ninian *Beyond Ideology*, 1981

Taylor, Charles *A Secular Age*, 2007

Toulmin, Stephen *The Return to Cosmology*, University of California Press, 1982

Tuan, Yi-Fu *Space and Place: the perspective of Experience*, University of Minnesota, 1977

Weil, Simone *The Need for Roots*, 1949

Wolin, R *The Politics of Being*, Columbia University, New York, 1990

Wyatt, Nicolas *The Mythic Mind: Essays on Cosmology and Religion in Ugaritic and Old Testament Literature*, 2005

Wyatt, Prof. N. 'Water, water everywhere... Musings on the Aqueous Myths of the Near East', Serie Proximo Antiguo, Zaragoza, 2003.

Wyatt, Prof. N. 'Sea and Desert: Symbolic Geography in West Semitic Religious Thought' Ugarit-Forschungen, vol 19, 1987.

Endnotes

[1] Bachelard, Gaston *The Poetics of Space*, 1958 (translated from the French by Maria Jolas in 1964), p5.

[2] Brooke, Rupert from 'The Soldier' published in 1915 in his book *1914 and Other Poems*.

[3] Nietzsche, Friedrich *The Joyful Wisdom*

[4] The distance to Andromeda, the nearest galaxy to our Milky Way is 2.5 million light years.

[5] See my *Through Mud and Barbed Wire* (2017), in which I examine the emotional and existential impact on Teilhard de Chardin of his theory of evolution towards a point Omega.

[6] 433 Eros is an asteroid of the Amor group, discovered by the German astronomer Carl Gustav Witt in 1898. It was visited by the NEAR Shoemacher space probe in 1998, orbited in 2000, with a soft landing on its surface in 2001. It became the first asteroid to be studied in this way.

[7] It is the second largest near-Earth object, the largest being 1036 Ganymed, with a diameter of about 20 miles.

[8] Taylor, Charles *A Secular Age*, 2007, p58

[9] Radford, Tim *The Consolations of Physics: Why the Wonders of the Universe Can Make You Happy*, reviewed by Graham Farmelo in *The Guardian*, Saturday 18th August 2018.

[10] For the purposes of this study, Camus should be considered an existentialist philosopher as well as a writer, although he distanced himself from the world of professional philosophy. We can also leave aside his dispute with Jean-Paul Sartre. What counts is that Camus deals with existential questions.

[11] Camus, Albert *The Myth of Sisyphus*

[12] In *The Sane Society*, originally published in 1955, see particularly chapter 3.

[13] Jaynes, Julian *The Origin of Consciousness in the Breakdown of the Bicameral Mind,* Penguin, 1976 p45f

[14] This pattern of mental operation is set out in, for example, the *Encyclopedia of Human Behaviour* (2nd edition, 2012).

[15] *Critique of Pure Reason*, AS1 B75.

[16] Einstein, Albert 'Science and Religion' an essay published in 1954.

[17] Wyatt, Nicolas *Space and Time in the Religious Life of the Ancient Near East*, p17.

[18] Heidegger, Martin *Bauen, Wohnen, Denken,* p378

[19] Wyatt, Nicolas *The Mythic Mind: Essays on Cosmology and Religion in Ugaritic and Old Testament Literature.*

[20] Wyatt (1999) "The Religion of Ugarit: An Overview," In: *Handbook of Ugaritic Stud*ies, ed. W.G.E.Watson & N. Wyatt, Brill, Leiden, p.529-585.

[21] See, for example, 'The cultural evolution of prosocial religions', by Ara Norenzayan and others, published in the journal *Behavioral and Brain Sciences* (2016).

[22] Wyatt, Nicolas *Space and Time in the Religious Life of the Ancient Near East*, p76.

[23] Eliade, Mircea *The Sacred and the Profane: the nature of religion* English translation 1959.

[24] Epicurus 'Letter to Herodotus' in a translation quoted in *Varieties of Unbelief*, edited by J. C. A. Gaskin, 1989.

[25] Lucretius, quoted in *Varieties of Unbelief*, edited by J. C. A. Gaskin, 1989.

[26] Mascall, Eric *Christian Theology and Natural Science.*

[27] Isaac Newton's *'The General Scholium'* was published alongside the second edition of his *Philosophiae Naturalis Principia Mathematica* in 1713.

[28] This phrase was used to introduce *Philosophers Behaving Badly*, Nigel Rodgers and Mel Thompson, Peter Owen, 2005

[29] Heidegger, Martin *Bauen, Wohnen, Denken* presented to the Darmstadt Symposium on 'Man and Space', August 5th 1951.

[30] *The Philosopher's Beach Book*, Hodder Education, 2012

[31] Collins, 1972, p167

[32] Gorner, Paul *Heidegger's Being and Time: an introduction*, CUP, 2007, p113–118.

[33] His reference to 'things in themselves' follows Kant's distinction between things in themselves (noumena) which are essentially unknowable, and our experience of those things (phenomena) which forms the limits of knowledge.

[34] Merleau-Ponty, M *Phenomenology of Perception* (translated by Colin Smith, 1962), p ix, but see also previous two pages.

[35] Published by the University of Minnesota Press.

[36] ibid page 136

[37] ibid p152

[38] Michel de Certeau *The Practice of Everyday Life*, University of California Press, 1984, see especially chapter IX.

[39] From *'Letter on Humanism'*

[40] Hierocles *Fragments, How we ought to conduct ourselves towards our kindred*

[41] From her Joseph Memorial Lecture, given at the Centre for Policy Studies in 1996.

[42] See, for example, *The English and Their History* by Robert Tombs, Alan Lane, 2014.

[43] Weil, Simone *The Need for Roots*, published in French in 1949 and in English in 1952. Routledge Classics edition, 2002, p 43.

[44] 'The Self-Affirmation of the German University' – Heidegger's rectoral address, delivered in 1933.

[45] For more background on Heidegger, including his flirtation with the Nazi party, see, for example, Rüdiger Safranski's *Martin Heidegger: Between Good and Evil*, 1998.

[46] For a discussion of the issues arising from Heidegger's view, see for example T*he Politics of Being* by Richard Wolin, Columbia University Press, 1990.

[47] See, for example, Peter Frankopan's *The Silk Roads: a New History of the World*, published in 2015.

[48] Lefebure, Henri *The Production of Space*, Blackwell, 1974 (English translation, 1991) outlines his contribution to this.

[49] The quotation is from the chapter 64 of the *Tao Te Jing*, where a journey begins either 'with the ground beneath your feet' or 'with a single step.' It is ascribed to Lao Tzu (an honorary title, meaning 'Old Master'), regarded as the founder of Taoist philosophy, and probably dating from the sixth century BCE.

[50] The words are taken from the opening of psalm 137.

[51] See, for example, *The Meaning of Friendship* by Mark Vernon, Palgrave Macmillan, 2006.

Index of Names

...

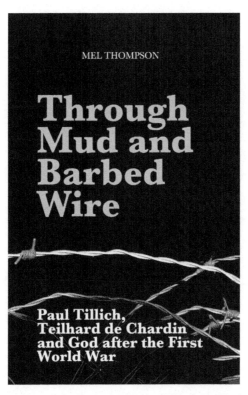

MEL THOMPSON

Through Mud and Barbed Wire

Paul Tillich, Teilhard de Chardin and God after the First World War

This is the story of two great religious thinkers, their response to the horrors of the Great War, and the impact it had on their lives and their ideas. The story moves from the trenches at Verdun, via theological discussions at Marburg, Tillich's expulsion by the Nazi regime and Teilhard's exile in China, to New York in the 1950s.

276 pages

ISBN: 9781979281034

Available in both e-book and paperback formats.

For more information, visit: www.philosophyandethics.com

...

Printed in Great Britain
by Amazon

11643189R00140